Ready-to-Use Activities for Teaching HAMLET

JOHN WILSON SWOPE

Ready-to-Use Activities for Teaching Teaching HAMLET

JOHN WILSON SWOPE

—◆—

THE CENTER FOR APPLIED
RESEARCH IN EDUCATION
West Nyack, New York 10995

Library of Congress Cataloging-in-Publication Data

Swope, John Wilson.
    Ready-to-use activities for teaching Hamlet / by John Wilson Swope.
      p.   cm. — (Shakespeare teacher's activities library)
    Includes bibliographical references.
    ISBN 0-87628-116-1
    1. Shakespeare, William, 1564-1616. Hamlet.   2. Shakespeare, William, 1564-
1616—Study and teaching (Secondary)   3. Activity programs in education.
I. Title.   II. Series: Swope, John Wilson.
Shakespeare teacher's activities library.
PR2807.S96   1994   93-39723
822.3'3—dc20   CIP

Printed in the United States of America

10 9 8 7 6 5 4 3

ISBN 0-87628-116-1

**THE CENTER FOR APPLIED RESEARCH
IN EDUCATION**
West Nyack, NY 10994

On the World Wide Web at http://www.phdirect.com

Dedication

To Noah

About the Author

In addition to eleven years as a middle and secondary English, speech, and drama teacher, John Wilson Swope has taught English education courses at the University of Florida and the University of Northern Iowa, where he is currently an assistant professor of English. His articles and reviews have appeared in *English Journal, English Leadership Quarterly, FOCUS, The Leaflet,* and *The Virginia English Bulletin.* He is a frequent presenter at conferences sponsored by the National Council of Teachers of English and its local affiliates. As an actor, director, and designer, he has participated in more than a dozen community theater productions.

About This Resource

Shakespeare's *Hamlet*, like *Romeo and Juliet*, *Julius Caesar*, and *Macbeth*, is a common choice for literature programs. As teachers, we enjoy these works and think them important for more than just their stories. For me, Shakespeare's ability to observe human nature and convey it through language commands my attention. His characters act and interact with others in ways that I recognize in those I meet. His poetry conveys human experience through timeless literary form.

Although we prize Shakespeare's plays, they present many problems for our students as first-time readers. We as teachers want our students to comprehend the plot, understand the motives of the characters, appreciate the language, and decipher countless allusions, often after only a single reading.

Before most students study *Hamlet*, they have already studied other plays, often either or both *Romeo and Juliet* and *Julius Caesar*. Even with this previous exposure to Shakespeare's plays, the students expect to have problems with Elizabethan language and conventions of blank verse; however, they possess the knowledge and personal experience that can help them understand and appreciate the play. Teenage readers can identify with many of the situations, characters, and themes within Shakespeare's *Hamlet*. Like Hamlet, many students experience the loss of a parent, whether through death or divorce, and the ambivalent emotions that accompany a parent's remarriage. Within their own school and community, they can identify persons who are skillful politicians like Claudius, those whose emotions control their lives like Ophelia, or those who often give advice to others, like Polonius. As teenagers, they know firsthand about struggles for power and autonomy. When we help students recall, organize, and share their relevant knowledge and experience, it becomes a valuable resource for them to begin understanding, appreciating, and interpreting the play.

As with other volumes in *Shakespeare Teacher's Activities Library*, *Ready-to-Use Materials for Hamlet* is a collection of student-centered activities for presenting the play to first-time readers. I've designed these activities to help students recall prior knowledge and personal experience that they can relate to the play. When students have little prior knowledge or experience that they can relate to the play, I have designed activities—such as the plot summaries, scenarios for improvisation, and prereading vocabulary help to "create" their knowledge.

Although students expect structure in a classroom, they tend to dislike a routine. This resource presents choices of activities to help students make connections between their lives and the play. The activities afford students opportunities to read, write, think, speak, and act out in response to *Hamlet*.

In developing these activities, I've drawn upon research in effective teaching, reading, whole language, and English education as well as my experience as a classroom teacher. I have also had the opportunities to team teach with my friends and colleagues, Sue Ellen Savereide, instructor at the Malcolm Price Laboratory

School, Cedar Falls, Iowa, and Sharon Palas, English teacher at Denver High School, Denver, Iowa. Their input has been invaluable in my developing these materials.

Although these activities will help get your students involved with *Hamlet*, I don't propose that these are the only ones that will work with students. As the teacher, you must determine which activities the students use, and whether or not they should work individually, in pairs, small groups, or as a whole class. You also need to decide whether the students should read silently, aloud, or in combination. I also encourage you to continue using the films and professional recordings of the play that have worked in the past, for both films and recordings may be used as prereading, reading, or postreading techniques. In addition to the ideas I present here, I urge you to develop your own specific improvisations, questions, and extending activities that reflect your specific teaching objectives, and that best fit your district's curriculum.

John Wilson Swope

Table of Contents

ACT III

PART ONE

——————— ❧ ———————

Suggestions to the Teacher

A Guide to Using This Resource

READING PROCESSES

In recent years, teachers have come to teach writing as a process of prewriting, writing, and rewriting. Approaching reading as a similar process of prereading, during-reading, and postreading allows students to assimilate difficult texts systematically, enhancing the students' comprehension, understanding, and appreciation. As a linguistic process, effective reading involves the reader: the reader anticipates what the text may reveal, reads to confirm or contradict those goals, and then thinks about what has been read.

To guide you in using reading as a process to teach *Hamlet*, this section will

- explain reading processes;
- establish a rationale for using a reading process approach to *Hamlet*;
- explain the overall organization of the student activities in this resource;
- explain the function of each of the various activities in this resource.

All activities follow a reading processes model and fall into the following three major groups, with a fourth group of optional activities called *extending activities*.

Prereading activities help students assess and organize information or personal experience that relates to what they will read. These activities help students to connect their prior knowledge to the text as well as help them to establish a genuine purpose for reading it.

During-reading activities encourage students to read actively rather than passively, taking more responsibility for their own learning. Because full comprehension of a text doesn't occur immediately upon reading it the first time, students often need help to make sense of what they've just read. By structuring reading sessions and using reading, writing, speaking, listening, viewing, and critical thinking activities to foster active contemplation of the text, students can begin to explore their possible interpretations of the text.

Postreading activities help students make sense of their earlier explorations of the literature and come to an overall understanding of a work.

Extending activities allow students to apply what they've learned about the text to new situations after they've reached an understanding of the work.

RATIONALE

Reading *Hamlet* is difficult, even for the most proficient students. As teachers, when we read the play along with our classes, we may be reading the text for the tenth or twentieth time. We may forget that our students are encountering this text for the first time. As teachers and students of literature ourselves, we have developed our appreciation, understanding, interpretations, and love of Shakespeare's plays through our repeated exposure to them. We have read, reread, contemplated, researched, discussed, listened to, and viewed performances of them. The activities in this resource apply a reading process approach to the study of *Hamlet* and encourage students to read, reread, contemplate, discuss, listen to, and view the play as active readers and learners, enhancing their understanding, appreciation, and enjoyment of it.

This resource provides you with choices of activities to help students understand *Hamlet*. The selection of activities depends upon the students you teach, your instructional goals, and the time you wish to devote to the study of the play. For example, a brief unit on *Hamlet* using these materials would include

- 🐚 completing one focusing activity and reviewing the plot summary for a specific scene as a prereading activity,
- 🐚 keeping either a character diary or a response journal throughout the reading of the play as a during-reading activity,
- 🐚 completing one of the postreading activities.

The vocabulary, viewing a scene on videotape, guides to character development, critical thinking questions, language exploration, and extending activities are other options to achieve additional instructional goals.

ORGANIZATION OF THE ACTIVITIES

To facilitate the planning of your unit, I've grouped the students' activities according to act. For each act, I've arranged the activities according to stage of the reading process: prereading, during-reading, postreading. (See Figure 1: Summary of Reading Process Activities for *Hamlet* located at the end of Part One.) Extending activities, designed for use only after a complete reading of the play, follow the materials for Act V. Answer keys for quizzes and suggested answers for discussion activities are located in Appendix C.

PREREADING ACTIVITIES

The prereading activities for *Hamlet* include focusing activities, vocabulary, and plot summaries.

Focusing Activities

All focusing activities share a common goal: to help students organize and apply relevant prior knowledge and experience to the scene they are about to read. Because these activities set the stage for reading, they should be brief, generally between five and ten minutes. These activities help establish a genuine purpose for reading by encouraging students to speculate about what *may* happen rather than to predict what eventually *does happen* in the play. Although several different focusing activities are available for each scene of the play, students need to complete *only one* of them: scenarios for improvisation, prereading discussion questions, speculation journal, or introducing the play with videotape.

Scenarios for Improvisation. These improvisational group activities take a few minutes for students to prepare and present but allow them to explore the possible motives and actions of the characters, in situations that relate to a particular scene. Once they present an improvisation to the class, it becomes a common experience and a part of each person's relevant prior knowledge. A brief discussion of the improvisation will help connect the improvisation to the action of the play. After reading, the students may wish to discuss the similarities between the improvisation and what actually occurred in the scene.

Prereading Discussion Questions. As an anticipatory device, these questions allow students to speculate about what they will read. The questions tend to be more effective once everyone has become familiar with the play and its characters.

Speculation Journal. This activity begins as an individual writing-to-learn activity. After students speculate for three to five minutes about what *might* happen, encourage them to share their predictions. Keep in mind that the goal is for them to use what they know about characters and motivations, to explore what *could* happen logically and not to guess correctly what *does* happen.

Introducing the Play with Videotape. Showing the opening scenes of a play before students begin reading it can be an excellent introductory focusing activity. A visual presentation provides them with a sense of the setting and overall action of the scene before they confront the written text. After showing the film or tape, ask the class, "What seems to be going on here?" A few minutes' discussion will help you determine if the class has a general sense of what they've seen.

Note that in the Zefferelli version with Mel Gibson, should you decide to use it, that in the first scene, the ghost does *not* appear. Instead the movie opens with the funeral of King Hamlet under the opening credits and then moves immediately to Claudius' speech in scene ii, which provides the exposition and establishes the conflict for the play.

Vocabulary

The vocabulary activities allow students to expand their vocabularies through repeated exposure to words within context. The words defined in the prereading lists are the bases for both of the postreading vocabulary activities: vocabulary in context and vocabulary review quiz. Although most of the words on these lists are in common use today, Shakespeare often used the words in different contexts than contemporary speakers do. The lists provide brief definitions and synonyms as well as a sentence to illustrate the word in a context similar to the one the students will encounter in the play.

Plot Summaries

Once students have completed a focusing activity, share the plot summary of the scene with them before they begin reading it. Reading the summary helps students establish the overall direction for the scene before beginning Shakespeare's verse. With the summary as a road map, students are less likely to get lost among Shakespeare's many literary allusions.

DURING-READING ACTIVITIES

Students need to read actively. When the text is as challenging as *Hamlet*, few students can comprehend it immediately. Instead, most of them need to contemplate the text consciously to make sense of it. During-reading activities allow them to re-read, write, talk, listen, view, and think about what they've just read.

Four types of activities enable students to contemplate actively what they've just read and begin to explore possible interpretations of it. These are: *response journal, character diary, viewing scenes on videotape,* and *guides to character development.*

Response Journal

This writing-to-learn activity is based upon the work of David Bleich. The students make four types of responses either while they read or immediately upon completing the reading of a particular scene. They respond emotionally to what they're reading and try to speculate why the text provokes a particular response. Then they record and explore their own associations and experiences that relate to the text. The figurative response then draws the students back to the text, making them contemplate an important section of it. Finally, the response journal encourages students to record the questions that arise while they read, so they can address them later.

All students keep an individual response journal throughout their reading of *Hamlet*. They use it as a means to record their reactions to what they read either while they read or immediately upon completing a reading session. For example, if students read the play aloud during class, encourage them to take the last few minutes of the period to write in their response journals. If students are to read outside of class, then also have them complete their response journals as part of the homework assignment. The writing in the response journal is exploratory in nature: it is a forum for formulating and testing hypotheses about the play, its language, and its characters; it is not a place where grammar, usage, and mechanics are an issue.

Character Diary

An alternative to the response journal, this exploratory writing-to-learn activity encourages students to read actively and to contemplate what they've read. The students summarize the action of the play, in the form of a personal diary, from the perspective of a minor character. Because no character is present for all the action of a play, the character diary requires students to provide a logical account of how their individual character comes to know the action. This paraphrasing not only improves the students' reading comprehension, but affects a broad range of related language skills, "including literal recall of events, characters, main points, rhetorical features, stylistic devices and text structure" (Brown and Cambourne, 9). Like the response journal, the writing in the character diary is exploratory in nature.

Viewing a Scene on Videotape

As an optional during-reading activity, students may view and discuss several scenes immediately after having read them. These include Claudius and Gertrude holding court (Act I, scene ii), Claudius' recruiting Rosencrantz and Guildenstern (Act II, scene ii), the court watching the traveling players (Act III, scene ii), Ophelia's madness (Act IV, scene v), and Hamlet and Laertes' duel (Act V, scene ii).

Because the students will already be familiar with the play's language, action, and characters, viewing the scene permits them to use the additional visual and auditory information to improve their understanding of the play's language and characters. For example, seeing a professional actor portray Claudius as he explains the death of his brother and his marriage to Gertrude demonstrates the rhetorical skill of a polished politician. Similarly, letting students see professional actors complete Hamlet and Laertes' duel in the closing scene may enhance their reading as well.

Guides to Character Development

These guides are additional, optional means to structure the students' contemplation of a play. Seven sets of guides to character development and revelation include Hamlet, Claudius, and Gertrude as major characters and Horatio, Laertes, Ophelia, and Polonius as minor ones.

How you use these activities depends on your specific goals for studying *Hamlet*. For example, you can have the entire class examine how Shakespeare develops a major character by having them choose to examine Hamlet, Gertrude, or Claudius. Similarly, they may examine how Shakespeare reveals minor and more static characters like Horatio or Polonius. Have them complete these activities individually, in pairs, or in small groups.

These charts direct students first to review specific portions of the play to determine what the characters do, say, or what other characters say about them before drawing conclusions about what insight this information provides for a specific character. You will find charts for the characters with the during-reading materials for each act in which the specific character appears. All the characters appear in Act I, while only Hamlet, Claudius, Gertrude, Ophelia, and Polonius appear in Act II. All but Laertes appear in Act III, and all except Polonius appear in Act IV. Only Hamlet, Claudius, Gertrude, Horatio, and Laertes appear in Act V.

POSTREADING ACTIVITIES

Postreading activities help students read, write, talk, or act their ways through the play to reach an overall understanding of it. This resource provides four types of postreading activities: *comprehension checks, critical thinking questions, language exploration,* and *vocabulary.*

Comprehension Checks

Two types of activities assess students' comprehension of the text they've read: a multiple choice quiz and small group discussion questions.

Comprehension Check (multiple choice). The quizzes consist of five multiple choice questions for each act. Two are factual, two are interpretative, and one is evaluative.

Small Group Discussion Questions to Check Comprehension. These questions help students assess whether or not they understand key issues of a play. Encourage them to discuss their answers with one another and return to the text to clarify misunderstandings through collaborative discussion in small groups.

Critical Thinking Questions

Postreading discussion questions are probably the most common activity found in literature classrooms. However, questions need to do more than simply check whether the students have read a particular passage. The Critical Thinking Questions follow the model of Christenbury and Kelly and help students connect the act that they've just read with the play as a whole, to their personal experiences, and to other literary experiences. To establish the goal for the discussion, present the focus question first. Although this question is the one that students will find difficult to answer at the onset, present it to them and just let them think about it. Explore the related issues in the other questions and then have the students return to the focus question to connect their other responses to it.

Language Exploration

These activities allow students to return to the text to explore how Shakespeare uses language within the context of the acts of the play that they've already read. Encourage them to use these activities to review and apply concepts and to develop interpretations of specific passages. The concepts in *Hamlet* include *figurative language* (*simile* and *metaphor*, *personification*, and *apostrophe*), *symbol*, *sensory imagery*, and *irony*.

Vocabulary Activities

Vocabulary in Context. For a postreading activity, students can examine how Shakespeare uses the prereading vocabulary within a specific passage. Then the students can apply an appropriate meaning and develop an interpretation of the passage within the context of the play. Although these activities direct students to excerpts, you can encourage students to review an entire passage of a particular scene to establish a more complete context.

Vocabulary Review Quizzes. These activities provide students with ways to assess their mastery of vocabulary for each act. The quiz items repeat deliberately, in modern language, the context established in the Vocabulary in Context activities. These quizzes are in a multiple-choice format to facilitate evaluation.

EXTENDING ACTIVITIES

Extending activities encourage students to apply what they've learned from studying *Hamlet* to alternative situations. They may complete these activities individually or in groups. This resource includes general directions for extending activities as well as more specific directions for acting out, oral interpretation, using puppet theater, making masks, and writing assignments.

Acting Out

Through improvisations, students can work out a skit to portray a particular scene or place a familiar character in a different context.

Oral Interpretation

These activities encourage students to present scenes from the play in its original language. With the suggested scenes, students can work either individually or in pairs. The directions include steps for preparing an effective oral interpretation. Students may wish to incorporate either puppet theater or masks into their presentations.

Puppet Theater

This activity includes directions for making paper bag puppets and suggestions for two, three, or more performers for specific scenes.

Paper Plate Masks

Masks provide a way to present visual interpretations of a character. Students can do this easily by constructing simple masks from paper plates as shown. These masks, like the puppets, may also be combined with oral or dramatic presentations.

Writing Assignments

Writing tasks give students a chance to incorporate their new understanding of the play into a piece of writing. To develop these assignments, they may want to use some of their reading process activities, such as response journals or character diaries, as sources for prewriting.

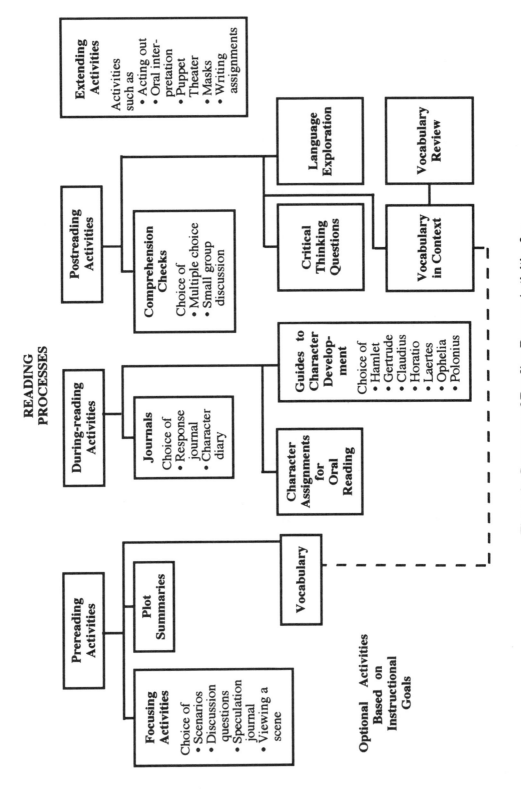

READING PROCESSES

Prereading Activities

Plot Summaries

Focusing Activities

Choice of
• Scenarios
• Discussion questions
• Speculation journal
• Viewing a scene

Vocabulary

Optional Activities Based on Instructional Goals

During-reading Activities

Journals

Choice of
• Response journal
• Character diary

Character Assignments for Oral Reading

Guides to Character Development

Choice of
• Hamlet
• Gertrude
• Claudius
• Horatio
• Laertes
• Ophelia
• Polonius

Postreading Activities

Comprehension Checks

Choice of
• Multiple choice
• Small group discussion

Language Exploration

Critical Thinking Questions

Vocabulary Review

Vocabulary in Context

Extending Activities

Activities such as
• Acting out
• Oral interpretation
• Puppet Theater
• Masks
• Writing assignments

Figure 1: Summary of Reading Process Activities for _Hamlet_

10

PART TWO

Ready-to-Use Materials for the Student

INTRODUCTORY MATERIALS
FOR
TEACHING SHAKESPEARE

William Shakespeare

©1994 by The Center for Applied Research in Education

William Shakespeare
April 23, 1564 — April 23, 1616

William Shakespeare was the eldest son and third child of John Shakespeare and Mary Arden. His father was a maker of white leather (whittawer) and gloves (glover), and a wool dealer as well as a yeoman farmer who owned his own land. As a prosperous and respected tradesman, John Shakespeare also took part in the local government of Stratford and held several government positions including Chamberlain (town treasurer), Alderman (town councilman), and Bailiff of Stratford-upon-Avon.

During William's childhood, Stratford was a prosperous, self-governing market town. As a result, the Corporation of Stratford maintained the grammar school originally founded by the medieval Gild of the Holy Cross where historians believe young William received his early education. The school's gildhall was also where traveling companies of actors probably performed. Records of the town suggest that William may have seen his first plays during his boyhood. The Chamberlain's accounts show that different companies of traveling players appeared and were paid from the borough's accounts on more than thirty occasions.

Town and church documents also show that William Shakespeare married Ann Hathaway when he was eighteen and she was twenty-six in 1582. They had three children, Susanna (1583) and twins Hamnet (1585–96) and Judith (1585–1662).

Shortly after his children were born, Shakespeare left Stratford and nothing is known of his life until he began acting in London in 1592. In London, he acted and served as a reviser and writer of plays. At age twenty-eight, he began to impress his contemporaries with the quality and popularity of his work. He published his first narrative poem, *Venus and Adonis* in 1593 and *The Rape of Lucrece* the following year.

While living in London, Shakespeare acted with several companies including the Chamberlain's Men (later called the King's Men) who provided entertainment for the Royal Court. He wrote many of his plays for his own acting company. Shakespeare was also partner in several theatrical ventures including being one of the proprietors of the Globe theater that was built just outside the city limits of London in 1599. His partners in the Globe also included famous actors of the time—Richard Burbage, Will Kempe, John Heminge, and Henry Condell. Heminge and Condell would publish the first collected editions of Shakespeare's plays, known as the First Folio, in 1623.

Although Shakespeare continued to live and work in London until 1610, he purchased New Place, one of the largest houses in Stratford in 1597. When he retired to New Place in 1610, he was a wealthy landowner whose estate included farmland, pasture, and gardens. Making occasional visits to London until 1614, Shakespeare continued to associate with actors and playwrights for the rest of his life. While in retirement at Stratford, he surrounded himself with family and friends.

Shakespeare died at home on April 23, St. George's Day in 1616. He was buried in the chancel of Holy Trinity Church in Stratford. He willed New Place to his elder daughter Susanna, then wife of Dr. John Hall. The poet's widow probably lived there with the Halls until her death in 1623. Within a few years of Shakespeare's death, a monument to him was erected and placed on the north wall of Westminster Abbey in London.

©1994 by The Center for Applied Research in Education

An Introduction to Shakespeare's Language

Because Shakespeare wrote nearly four hundred years ago, some of the conventions that he uses in his plays present problems for modern readers. Most of Shakespeare's lines are written in poetry. Although these lines don't usually rhyme, they do have a set rhythm (called *meter*). To achieve the meter, Shakespeare arranges words so that the syllables, which are stressed or said more loudly than others, fall in a regular pattern: dah DUM dah DUM dah DUM dah DUM dah DUM. For example, read the following lines from *Hamlet* aloud:

❧

Neither a borrower nor a lender be,
For loan oft loses both itself and friend.

❧

Because you are familiar with the words that Shakespeare uses here, you naturally stressed every second syllable:

❧

nei THER a BOR rower NOR a LEN der BE,
for LOAN oft LO ses BOTH it SELF and FRIEND.

❧

The pattern of one unstressed syllable followed by a stressed one, dah DUM, is called an *iamb*. Each pattern is referred to as a *foot*. Because Shakespeare uses five iambic feet to a line, this pattern in known as *iambic pentameter*.

In order for Shakespeare to maintain the set meter of most lines, he often structures the lines differently than normal English speech. He may change the normal order of words so that the stressed syllables fall in the appropriate place. For example, the following sentence has no set meter:

❧

You WON'T GO till I SET up a GLASS for YOU.

❧

However, Shakespeare turns these words around a bit to maintain the meter in *Hamlet*:

17

He may also shorten words by omitting letters so that a two-syllable word is one syllable. As a result, *over* often appears as *o'er* and *'tis* in place of *it is*.

Shakespeare also uses forms of words that we rarely use today, nearly four hundred years later. Among these are the personal pronouns *thou* (you), *thine* (your, yours), *thee* (you as in "to you"), and *thyself* (yourself). Often Shakespeare also uses verb endings that we no longer use. For example, *hath* is an old form of *has*, and *art* an older form of *are*. You're also likely to encounter several words or phrases that we no longer use at all: *anon* instead of *soon*, or *shortly* or *prithee* meaning *I pray to thee (you)*.

NAME:_____   DATE:_____

Conventions of Shakespeare's Staging

When we attend theatrical performances—school plays, assembly programs, or movies in public theaters—we're accustomed to finding a seat and waiting until the lights dim, the audience quiets down, and the play or feature begins. We're also used to seeing scenery that suggests the location of the play and expect the stage lighting to help set the mood.

But all this was not so in Shakespeare's time. Then people attended plays during the day, for there was no way to light the stage effectively once the sun had set. Public performance of plays in theaters was a fairly new idea at the time because the first permanent English theater had been built less than twenty years before Shakespeare began writing his plays. Although the shape of the theaters varied from square, circular, or octagon, all had a stage that was simply a raised platform in an open yard surrounded with tiers of galleries to accommodate the spectators. The stage was covered with a roof, commonly called "The Heavens." While the roof protected the actors from the weather, the attic space above could hold machinery, such as ropes and pulleys to lower thrones or heavenly deities to the stage or to hide the sound effects of thunder, alarum bells, or cannonades. By modern standards these theaters were small. The open yard in front of the stage in one theater measured only fifty-five feet across. Up to two thousand spectators could either sit on benches in the tiers of galleries or stand in the open yard in front of the stage.

These theaters used simple stage props—chairs or tables were brought on the raised platform as needed. Actual scenery may have been suggested through dialogue or may have included minimal set pieces such as a few trees to suggest a forest, or a rock to suggest a river bank. The stages themselves had many built-in acting areas that could function in a number of ways: for instance, small inner stages with drapes which the actors used as inner rooms, or raised balconies. The actors could use the inner room for King Duncan's chamber in *Macbeth* or Brutus' tent in *Julius Caesar*. The balcony might serve as Juliet's balcony in *Romeo and Juliet* or as the battlements of Elsinore Castle in *Hamlet*.

The costumes were based on the contemporary clothing styles of the time. Instead of attempting any sort of accurate historical costuming, the actors wore clothes much like those of a character's rank. For example, Macbeth would have been costumed as any nobleman and Lady Capulet as any wealthy English merchant's wife. Occasionally, other costume pieces may have been added to suggest witches, fairies, national or racial costumes.

During the time that Shakespeare wrote and acted, only three or four professional companies performed in theaters just outside the limits of London. These professional troupes employed only male actors. Although most of the roles in Shakespeare's plays are male, the few parts of younger female characters—like Ophelia or Juliet, for instance—were played by young boys, aged fourteen or so and apprenticed to actors. Men may have played some female roles, especially those of older, comedic women, such as Juliet's Nurse.

Principal Locations for <u>Hamlet</u>

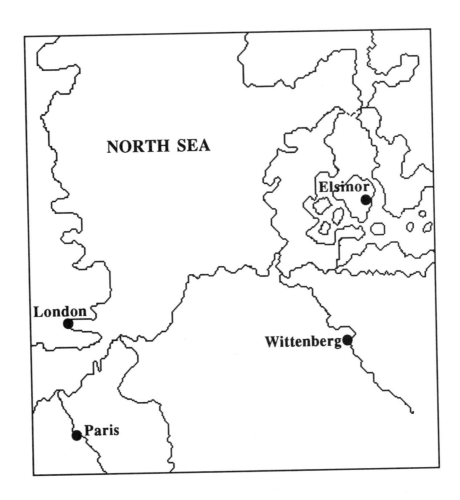

ACT I

Focusing Activities
for
Hamlet
Scenarios for Improvisation
Act I

Directions: Presented below are locations and situations involving characters. As your teacher directs you, but before reading an individual scene, pretend to be one of the characters and act out the situation. Don't worry about speaking like characters in Shakespeare's plays, just try to imagine how you would react to the situation and use your own language. Your teacher may give you a few minutes to discuss what you would like to do with the other performers. Your teacher will probably ask you to act out your scene for others in the class. When you finish, your teacher may ask your classmates to discuss what they've seen.

scene i. *Scene*: An abandoned house in a remote area of town, Halloween night.

Characters: Nick, Chris, Jesse.

Situation: Nick and Jesse claim to have seen a ghost appear in the house at midnight on the preceding two nights. Chris, who is known to be logical and skeptical, has come to see for herself/himself. When the ghost does appear, how does it affect everyone?

scene ii. *Scene*: The Royal Court.

Characters: Claudius, Hamlet, Gertrude.

Situation: Claudius, Hamlet's uncle, has succeeded to the throne following the strange death of Hamlet's father, King Hamlet. In addition to Claudius becoming king, he has also married Gertrude, Hamlet's mother. Claudius and Gertrude are appearing for the first time as King and Queen. How do they explain their hasty marriage and how does Hamlet react?

scene iii. *Scene:* Polonius' house.

Characters: Laertes, Ophelia, Polonius.

Situation: Laertes is going away to college. He has come to say goodbye to his younger sister who is in love for the first time. What advice does he give her? When their father, Polonius, comes in, what advice does he give to his son?

23

Focusing Activities
for
Hamlet
Small Group Discussion Questions
Act I

Directions: Before reading scenes in Act I, discuss the questions in small groups. You may want to make notes about your discussion so you can share them with classmates or refer back to them after you've read the scene.

scene i.

1. Based upon what you may have heard or seen, what do you think happens in the play, *Hamlet*?

2. What character traits do you feel permit a national leader like the President of the United States to be popular? What character traits do you feel permit a national leader to be effective? What can a national leader do to be both popular and effective?

scene ii.

1. If your father had died only a few months ago, how do you think you'd react to your mother remarrying? How would your feelings change if your mother married your father's brother, your uncle?

2. If you had just seized power of a small but powerful country, what would you do to secure your position as President?

scene iii.

1. If you were a young man going back to college, what advice would you give to your teenage sister about boys and dating?

2. If you were a father, what advice would you give your son before sending him off to college?

scenes iv and v.

1. Do you think that the ghost is the spirit of Hamlet's dead father or an evil spirit? What evidence can you cite to justify your choice?

2. What do you think the ghost will tell Hamlet?

Focusing Activities
for
Hamlet
Speculation Journal
Act I

Directions: This activity is to help you become involved actively with reading the play by helping you to determine a definite purpose for reading. Before you read these scenes in Act I, take a few minutes to respond in writing to the questions below. Don't worry about correct answers here. Use your own experience, what you know, or what you may have heard about the play to speculate about what you think might happen. Sometimes, as for scenes i, ii, and iii below, you may be asked to speculate about issues that parallel the action of the play. After reading a scene, you may find that the characters reacted differently than you thought. Don't worry about these differences; just make note of them because you will have opportunities to share these differences in other activities.

**scenes
i and ii.**

1. Based upon what you have seen or heard, what do you expect *Hamlet* to be about?

2. What do you think of a person who would assassinate his brother, seize the throne, and then marry his widowed former sister-in-law?

3. As heir to the throne, how do you think this series of events would affect your relationships with both your mother and uncle?

scene iii.

1. What advice would you expect an older brother to give his teenage sister about boys and dating before the brother went off to college?

2. What advice would you expect a father to give his son before sending him off to college?

scenes iv and v.

1. If the ghost is an evil spirit, what do you expect it to tell Hamlet?

2. If the ghost is indeed the spirit of Hamlet's father, what do you think it will tell Hamlet?

After Reading Act I: Now that you have finished reading Act I, which of your speculations were most accurate? How do you account for them? Which ones were least like the action of the play? Why do you think you speculated as you did?

Focusing Activity
for
Hamlet
Introducing the Play with Videotape

Directions: Before you begin reading *Hamlet*, you will view a video version of the opening scenes. Don't worry about trying to understand everything, just go for general impressions. As you watch, you may want to note questions you would like to ask your teacher afterwards. After viewing the scene, take a few minutes to respond to the questions below.

1. In your own words, briefly describe what you saw. What seems to be the overall conflict or problem?

2. Where does the scene take place? Which particular details help you to understand the action?

3. What kinds of things can the director of the film or video version do in this scene that a director could not do in a production of a stage play?

NAME:_____   DATE:_____

Prereading Activity
for
Hamlet
Vocabulary
Act I

Directions: Shakespeare uses the following words in Act I. The section below provides a brief definition of each word and provides a sentence to illustrate its meaning. You may wish to review the words for a particular scene immediately before reading it.

Definitions.

scene i

1. **emulate:** (adj.) ambitious, rivalrous.
   Example: As an *emulate* character, Shakespeare has Claudius murder his brother, King Hamlet, before the beginning of the play.

2. **harrow:** (v.) to cause extreme distress of mind or emotions; to vex.
   Example: The sudden death of Jan's grandfather *harrowed* his emotions.

3. **shark:** (v.) to prey upon; to gather together for booty or gain.
   Example: The gang *sharked* together on the corner and then decided to loot the store.

scene ii

4. **tenable:** (adj.) capable of being held or retained.
   Example: After the general surveyed the areas for natural fortifications carefully, he determined the fort was *tenable*.

scene iii

5. **necessary:** (n.) a necessity.
   Example: Food, clothing, and shelter are *necessaries* for life.

6. **credent:** (adj.) believing or willing to believe.
   Example: My nephew is too *credent* of the claims of television advertisers.

7. **husband-ry:** (n.) management, thrift.
   Example: Environmentalists have made most of us more aware of the *husbandry* of our natural resources.

scene iv

8. **shrewdly:** (adj.) sharply, intensely, grievously.
   Example: The mother's sarcastic remark to her son after he missed the catch criticized his performance in the game *shrewdly*.

9. **eager:** (adj.) sour, acid, or bitter.
   Example: Losing the championship basketball game by one point in the last few seconds was an *eager* disappointment for the whole team.

10. **hearse:** (v.) to lay on a bier or in a coffin; to bury with funeral rites and ceremony.
    Example: The body of Queen Elizabeth I is *hearsed* in a stone tomb in Westminster Abbey.

Prereading Activity
for
Hamlet
Plot Summaries
Act I

Directions: To help you better understand and follow *Hamlet*, read the summary of a specific scene before you begin to read it. If you get lost during the scene, you can refer to the summary.

Act I, scene i

Guards on the battlements of Elsinore Castle claim to have seen a ghost appear at night. Although Horatio has suggested to them that it is only their imaginations, they ask him to wait for it again. While they wait, they tell Horatio what they've seen. Suddenly the ghost of Hamlet, former king of Denmark, appears, and they urge Horatio to speak to it, but it vanishes without answering. Horatio, shaken by what he's seen, interprets the ghost's presence as a bad omen for the country.

Marcellus then asks for information about Denmark's recent preparations for war. Horatio reports that Fortinbras, Prince of Norway, is again raising an army to retake the territory that his father, King Fortinbras, lost in an earlier war to King Hamlet.

Horatio reminds the group that Julius Caesar's ghost had appeared as a warning to the Romans, and when the ghost of Hamlet returns and gestures to the group, Horatio again addresses it, hoping that it will speak, asking whether it has unfinished business or brings a warning. Before the ghost can speak, the rooster crows and the ghost vanishes. All decide to tell Prince Hamlet what they've seen, to see if the ghost will speak to him.

Act I, scene ii

The next morning, Claudius and Gertrude hold court officially as the new King and Queen of Denmark. In the opening speech, Claudius refers to his brother's death and explains his marriage to Gertrude, his brother's widow. Claudius then explains how he plans to deal with Fortinbras, Prince of Norway. Fortinbras, hoping to take advantage of King Hamlet's death and the subsequent disorder that might follow it, has requested the Danes surrender the lands that King Hamlet had taken from the Norwegians. Instead, Claudius writes to Fortinbras' uncle, the King of Norway, informing him of his nephew's quest for power and asking that the King curtail Fortinbras' power for the present.

Claudius then turns to Laertes. Laertes wishes to return to France, but needs the King's permission to leave the court. Because Polonius, Laertes' father, has reluctantly granted permission for him to go, Claudius also grants his permission.

Claudius now turns to Hamlet. Both Gertrude and Claudius urge Hamlet to accept his father's death as part of the natural cycle of life. Hamlet's reply is that he is not playing but actually continuing to mourn his father's death. Gertrude then asks Hamlet to remain at court rather than return to his studies at Wittenberg.

Once Hamlet is alone, he reveals in soliloquy that he is discouraged and weary of the recent events in his world: his father's death and his mother's marriage to his uncle less than two months later.

Horatio, Marcellus, and Barnardo tell Hamlet about the ghost. Hamlet vows to go see it for himself and to talk with it.

Act I, scene iii

In Polonius' house a short while later, Laertes prepares to return to France. After he says goodbye to his sister Ophelia, he advises her on her relationship with Hamlet. He tells her that Hamlet's attentions may be just a passing phase, and she should be careful not to fall in love with him. Laertes also reminds his sister that because Hamlet is heir to the throne of Denmark he is not always free to choose his life and how he will live it.

Polonius enters and encourages his son to be off, for the winds won't wait. Before Laertes leaves, Polonius offers him advice about how to conduct himself. Look at a person's character. Be friendly but not common. Be loyal to your friends. Don't live only for entertainment. Don't get drawn into quarrels. Listen to another's opinions and problems, but give few of your opinions or confidences. Dress as well as you can afford but not unnecessarily showy, and don't lend or borrow money from friends.

As Laertes leaves, he reminds Ophelia of his advice. When Polonius asks his daughter to explain what Laertes means, Ophelia tells him that the advice was about Hamlet. Polonius shares that he has heard that she and Hamlet have been spending a lot of time together recently. He suggests that she should spend less time with him. When Ophelia tries to convince her father of Hamlet's sincerity, Polonius replies that she should be all the more skeptical about his motives. Hamlet, as a young man, may have more experience than she does. He may only be trying to seduce her. He asks that she not see Hamlet for the present. Ophelia promises to obey.

Act I, scene iv

About midnight, Hamlet keeps watch with his friends Horatio and Marcellus on the battlements, hoping to see the ghost. While they wait, they hear the noise of Claudius and the court partying below. The noise causes Hamlet to reflect that a single flaw can ruin the reputation of a person, and the character of an entire nation.

When the ghost appears, Hamlet insists upon speaking to it directly and referring to it as the ghost of his father. The ghost beckons Hamlet to come with it, as though to speak in private. Although Horatio urges Hamlet not to go, for the ghost may be an evil spirit that could lure Hamlet to his death, Hamlet and the ghost retire to another part of the battlement.

After Hamlet goes, Horatio interprets the presence of the ghost as an omen that "something is rotten in the state of Denmark."

*Act I,
scene v*

Once Hamlet is alone with the ghost, he demands that it speak.

The ghost identifies itself as his father, and tells Hamlet of his fate and the truth about how he died. The ghost explains that he is doomed to wander the night while he spends the day burning away the crimes he had committed in life. Although the ghost could tell Hamlet frightening stories, he doesn't have time. The ghost asks Hamlet to take revenge upon his murderer.

The ghost informs Hamlet that the story that Claudius has told about how King Hamlet died is a lie. According to Claudius' account, the King, while taking a nap in his orchard, was bitten on the ear by a poisonous snake. In reality, Claudius, who lusted after Gertrude, sneaked up on his sleeping brother and poured poison into the king's ear, killing him. With the king dead, Claudius could marry Gertrude and take the throne for himself.

Once Hamlet hears the ghost's story, it confirms his suspicions about Claudius and Gertrude. He promises the ghost that he will avenge the murder. The ghost then vanishes.

When Horatio and Marcellus find Hamlet, they want to know what happened. Hamlet makes his friends vow the secrets that he has learned. He also tells them that no matter how strange his behavior becomes, that he will only pretend to be insane. In the future, they should not reveal that he has talked with the ghost of his father that night. They swear on Hamlet's sword not to tell what they have seen.

Class Period:

CHARACTER ASSIGNMENTS FOR ORAL READING GROUPS
Hamlet

Session 1: Act I, scenes i, ii

Characters	*Group 1*	*Group 2*	*Group 3*	*Group 4*
Francisco, Claudius	___	___	___	___
Barnardo, Cornelius, and Voltemand	___	___	___	___
Horatio	___	___	___	___
Marcellus	___	___	___	___
Laertes	___	___	___	___
Gertrude	___	___	___	___
Hamlet	___	___	___	___
Polonius	___	___	___	___

34

Class Period:

CHARACTER ASSIGNMENTS FOR ORAL READING GROUPS
Hamlet

Session 2: Act I, scenes iii, iv, v

Characters	*Group 1*	*Group 2*	*Group 3*	*Group 4*
Hamlet (scene iv)	___	___	___	___
Hamlet (scene v)	___	___	___	___
Horatio	___	___	___	___
Marcellus	___	___	___	___
Ghost	___	___	___	___
Polonius	___	___	___	___
Laertes	___	___	___	___
Ophelia	___	___	___	___

35

During-reading Activity
for
Hamlet
Directions for Response Journal

Although we often read silently, reading is an active process. As we run our eyes across a line of text, we transform the letters and words into mental images. The words have the power to affect us in many ways. The purpose of this response journal is to help you as a reader verbalize several different types of responses immediately after you've read, and to assist you in recalling the experiences of reading prior to discussing them with your classmates.

Your response journal is a place for you to react to what you read personally. This is also a place to begin piecing together your understanding of the play. Your journal is a place to think aloud on paper and not have to worry about grammatical correctness or punctuation. You may wish to do it as you read or immediately upon finishing a reading session. It won't be nearly as effective if you put it off! There are four types of responses you should make each time. None of these needs to be more than a brief paragraph, four paragraphs total.

1. *Respond emotionally.* How does the play make you feel at this point? Record your responses in a few sentences and then explore them for a few minutes, trying to figure out why you feel as you do.

2. *Make associations between ideas in the text and your personal experience.* In what situations have you felt similar to the characters? What persons, places, or ideas from your own experiences came to your mind while you were reading this portion of the play? Try to list three to five associations, but don't worry about trying to figure out why they came to mind. Just accept that they occur.

3. *Look at the language.* What portions of Shakespeare's language attracts your attention? These might be individual words, phrases, lines, scenes, or images. Make note of whatever feature(s) draw your attention. Speculate for a few minutes about what you think these might mean.

4. *Record any questions or problems.* Make note of any portion of the play, its language, or events that seem to cause you problems. Write down any questions that occur to you as you read.

Here's a sample journal for Act I, scene i:

1. The soldiers, Barnardo, Francisco, and Marcellus sure do seem superstitious. They seem willing to believe almost anything. Horatio seems smarter somehow. I wonder how the ghost could be both more ghostly and at the same time represent a physical presence on stage?

2. This opening scene reminds me of some stereotypical opening shot for a horror movie—lightning, storm coming around a spooky castle.

    Sounds sort of like the setting for a Halloween prank like in "The Legend of Sleepy Hollow."
    These guys seem as afraid as most little kids are when they go see a horror movie like either the "Halloween" or "Nightmare on Elm Street" series.
    The ghost may live in another dimension like the ones depicted in the movies "Ghost" or "Beetlejuice."

3. When Horatio says, "I'll cross it, though it blast me," it seems like he's suggesting both making the sign of the cross against the ghost to protect himself and confronting the ghost at the same time.

4. What would make the soldiers believe that the ghost is an evil spirit?

NAME:_____   DATE:_____

During-reading Activity
for
Hamlet
Response Journal

Directions: Use the spaces below to record your responses to the act and scenes of *Hamlet* that you've just finished reading. Respond in all four ways and take a few additional minutes to explore why you think you responded as you did.

Response Journal for Act ___, scene ____ to Act ___, scene ___.

1. How does the play make you feel at this point? Record your emotional response(s) in a few sentences and then explore them for a few minutes, trying to figure out why you feel as you do.

2. In what situations have you felt similar to the characters ? What persons, places, or ideas from your own experiences came to your mind while you were reading this portion of the play? Try to list at least three associations, but don't worry about trying to figure out why they came to mind. Just accept that they occur.

   a.

   b.

   c.

3. What portions of Shakespeare's language attracts your attention? These might be individual words, phrases, lines, scenes, or images. Make note of whatever features draw your attention. Speculate for a few minutes about what you think they might mean.

4. Make note of any portion of the play, its language, or events that cause you problems. Note any questions that you might ask.

During-reading Activity
for
Hamlet
Directions for Character Diary

As you read *Hamlet*, you will find that the events of the play affect the lives of all the characters, not just Hamlet. To give you an opportunity to explore the reactions of other characters, pretend to be one of the characters listed below. For this assignment, you will keep the personal diary of a single character.

Select one of the following characters for your diary:

Hamlet, Prince of Denmark	Horatio
Gertrude, Queen of Denmark	Claudius, King of Denmark
Laertes	Fortinbras, Prince of Norway
Cornelius or Voltemand, Claudius' ambassadors	The Gravedigger (*see* Act V, scene i)
The Sexton (*see* Act V, scene i)	Marcellus

In your diary, summarize the events of the act and provide an explanation for how your character may have heard of them if the character was not involved with the events directly, and react as your character would. For example, Laertes, Ophelia's brother, leaves for France after appearing in scenes ii and iii of Act I and then reappears in scenes v and vii of Act IV and in all of Act V. Although he is not present, he would logically have friends and family who send him letters and keep him informed about what is happening at the court of King Claudius and Queen Gertrude. Here is a sample of what his diary might look like after reading Act I, scene i:

Now that King Claudius is crowned and he and Gertrude have married, I can get back to school in Paris. Life is much too tame around here. I miss the company of my friends and the challenge of my teachers. My valet tells me that Bernardo and Marcellus have supposedly sighted a ghost during their nightly watch on the battlements, but we all know how superstitious soldiers can be. It's probably just an hallucination. We all know that King Hamlet died from a poisonous snake bite.

Unlike other plays by Shakespeare that you may have studied, there is little evidence within the play to tie the action to a specific time of the year. All the action takes place in and around Elsinor Castle.

© 1994 by The Center for Applied Research in Education

Use the following summary of events to help you keep your character diary for *Hamlet:*

Acts and Scenes	Time and Place
Act I, scene i	Midnight on the battlements of the castle
Act I, scenes ii and iii	The next day
Act I, scenes iv and v	The following night
Act II, scenes i and ii	Six or eight weeks later
Act III, scenes i	The next day
Act III, scenes ii, iii, iv	That evening
Act IV, scenes i, ii, iii, iv	The same evening, immediately following
Act IV, scenes v, vi, vii	A few weeks later
Act V, scenes i, ii	Four or five days later

NAME:_____   DATE:_____

During-reading Activity
for
Hamlet
Character Diary 1
Act I, scenes i and ii

Directions: Use the space below to record your character's reactions to the events of the first two scenes in Act I of *Hamlet*. Remember to include a summary of events, explain how your character learned of them, and give your character's reactions to them. Because this act has five scenes, you may wish to record your character's entries as you read each scene. If you need additional room, use the back of this sheet.

The Personal Diary of

_____
(character's name)

Early morning (scene i)

_____

_____

_____

_____

_____

_____

Later (scene ii)

_____

_____

_____

_____

_____

_____

NAME:_____   DATE:_____

During-reading Activity
for
Hamlet
Character Diary 2
Act I, scenes iii, iv, v

Directions: Use the space below to record your character's reactions to the events of the last three scenes in Act I of *Hamlet*. Remember to include a summary of events, explain how your character learned of them, and give your character's reactions to them. Because this act has five scenes, you may wish to record your character's entries as you read each scene. If you need additional room, use the back of this sheet.

The Personal Diary of

_____
(character's name)

Late afternoon (scene iii)

_____

_____

_____

_____

_____

_____

Midnight or early morning (scenes iv and v)

_____

_____

_____

_____

_____

_____

During-reading Activity
for
Hamlet
Viewing Act I, scene ii
Claudius and Gertrude Hold Court

Directions: After you've read this scene, viewing a film or video version may help you better understand how the text translates into the characters' actions. Although you may want to keep your copy of the play handy, don't be surprised if the actors' script varies from yours. Film scripts often delete or reorder the lines in the play. You many want to note questions you need to ask your teacher afterwards. After viewing the scene, take a few minutes to respond to the questions below.

1. What do the costumes and the set, which represent the Danish Royal Court, tell you about the time of the play?

2. What business must Claudius attend to during this scene?

3. What seems to be Hamlet's attitude towards Claudius and the recent changes in his life? What seems to motivate Claudius and how does he regard Gertrude?

4. How do the actor's facial expressions, tones of voice, and gestures enhance Shakespeare's words?

NAME:_____   DATE:_____

During-reading Activity
for
Hamlet
Guide to Character Development: Hamlet
Act I

Shakespeare reveals his characters in four ways:

🙡 through what the characters say to other characters in dialogue;

🙡 through what the characters reveal about their thoughts through long speeches to the audience called *soliloquies*;

🙡 through what other characters say about them;

🙡 through what they do, their actions.

As you read the play, examine the following scenes for what they reveal about Hamlet's character and briefly fill in the chart using your own words. If you need more room, use the back of the page.

Scene	What Hamlet says, does, or what others say about him	What this reveals about Hamlet's character
Act I, scene ii Claudius' statement about the death of King Hamlet and the remarriage of Queen Gertrude		
Act I, scene ii Claudius and Gertrude's attempts to address Hamlet's melancholy behavior		
Act I, scene ii Hamlet's soliloquy ("O that this too too solid flesh would melt . . . ")		

Scene	What Hamlet says, does, or what others say about him	What this reveals about Hamlet's character
Act I, scene ii Horatio and the others tell Hamlet about the ghost		
Act I, scene iv The revelry of the court in the castle below the basement		
Act I, scene iv The ghost appears		
Act I, scene v The ghost speaks to Hamlet		

During-reading Activity
for
Hamlet
Guide to Character Development: Gertrude
Act I

Shakespeare reveals his characters in four ways:

◊ through what the characters say to other characters in dialogue;

◊ through what the characters reveal about their thoughts through long speeches to the audience called *soliloquies*;

◊ through what other characters say about them;

◊ through what they do, their actions.

As you read the play, examine the following scene for what it reveals about Gertrude's character and fill in the chart briefly using your own words. If you need more room, use the back of the page.

Scene	What Gertrude says, does, or what others say about her	What this reveals about Gertrude's character
Act I, scene ii Claudius and Gertrude's attempts to address Hamlet's melancholy behavior		

During-reading Activity
for
Hamlet
Guide to Character Development: Claudius
Act I

Shakespeare reveals his characters in four ways:

❧ through what the characters say to other characters in dialogue;

❧ through what the characters reveal about their thoughts through long speeches to the audience called *soliloquies*;

❧ through what other characters say about them;

❧ through what they do, their actions.

As you read the play, examine the following scenes for what they reveal about Claudius' character and fill in the chart briefly using your own words. If you need more room, use the back of the page.

Scene	What Claudius says, does, or what others say about him	What this reveals about Claudius' character
Act I, scene ii Claudius' statement about the death of King Hamlet and the remarriage of Queen Gertrude		
Act I, scene ii Claudius and Gertrude's attempts to address Hamlet's melancholy behavior		

NAME:_____   DATE:_____

During-reading Activity
for
Hamlet
Guide to Character Development: Horatio
Act I

Shakespeare reveals his characters in four ways:

&❧ through what the characters say to other characters in dialogue;

&❧ through what the characters reveal about their thoughts through long speeches to the audience called *soliloquies*;

&❧ through what other characters say about them;

&❧ through what they do, their actions.

As you read the play, examine the following scenes for what they reveal about Horatio's character and fill in the chart briefly using your own words. If you need more room, use the back of the page.

Scene	What Horatio says, does, or what others say about him	What this reveals about Horatio's character
Act I, scene i Bernardo, Marcellus, and Francisco tell Horatio they've seen a ghost		
Act I, scene i Horatio and the others see the ghost		
Act I, scene ii Horatio and the others tell Hamlet about the ghost		
Act I, scene iv The ghost appears		

Scene	What Horatio says, does, or what others say about him	What this reveals about Horatio's character
Act I, scene v The ghost speaks to Hamlet		
Act I, scene v Hamlet tells Horatio and the others about the ghost		

During-reading Activity
for
Hamlet
Guide to Character Development: Laertes
Act I

Shakespeare reveals his characters in four ways:

  ❧ through what the characters say to other characters in dialogue;

  ❧ through what the characters reveal about their thoughts through long speeches to the audience called *soliloquies*;

  ❧ through what other characters say about them;

  ❧ through what they do, their actions.

As you read the play, examine the following scenes for what they reveal about Laertes' character and fill in the chart briefly using your own words. If you need more room, use the back of the page.

Scene	*What Laertes says, does, or what others say about him*	*What this reveals about Laertes' character*
Act I, scene ii Laertes' request to return to Paris		
Act I, scene iii Hamlet's wooing of Ophelia		
Act I, scene iii His father's advice before leaving		

© 1994 by The Center for Applied Research in Education

During-reading Activity
for
Hamlet
Guide to Character Development: Ophelia
Act I

Shakespeare reveals his characters in four ways:

❧ through what the characters say to other characters in dialogue;

❧ through what the characters reveal about their thoughts through long speeches to the audience called *soliloquies*;

❧ through what other characters say about them;

❧ through what they do, their actions.

As you read the play, examine the following scene for what it reveals about Ophelia's character and fill in the chart briefly using your own words. If you need more room, use the back of the page.

Scene	What Ophelia says, does, or what others say about her	What this reveals about Ophelia's character
Act I, scene iii Laertes' advice about Hamlet's wooing of Ophelia		
Polonius' response to Hamlet's wooing of Ophelia		

© 1994 by The Center for Applied Research in Education

NAME:_____ DATE:_____

During-reading Activity
for
Hamlet
Guide to Character Development: Polonius
Act I

Shakespeare reveals his characters in four ways:

🎜 through what the characters say to other characters in dialogue;

🎜 through what the characters reveal about their thoughts through long speeches to the audience called *soliloquies*;

🎜 through what other characters say about them;

🎜 through what they do, their actions.

As you read the play, examine the following scenes for what they reveal about Polonius' character and fill in the chart briefly using your own words. If you need more room, use the back of the page.

Scene	What Polonius says, does, or what others say about him	What this reveals about Polonius' character
Act I, scene ii Laertes' request to return to Paris		
Act I, scene iii Polonius' advice to Laertes		
Hamlet's wooing of Ophelia		

Postreading Activity
for
Hamlet
Comprehension Check
Act I

Directions: After you've read all of Act I, use the following questions to check how well you've understood what you've read. For each question, select the most appropriate answer from the choices listed. Place the letter corresponding to your answer in the space to the left of the item number.

_____1. Although the ghost wants Hamlet to take revenge upon Claudius, Hamlet believes he needs additional proof of Claudius' guilt because

  A. Claudius may be Hamlet's natural father.
  B. Polonius advises Hamlet to get further evidence before accusing the present king.
  C. taking revenge will spoil Hamlet's plans to marry Ophelia.
  D. the ghost may be an evil spirit.
  E. Hamlet suspects Gertrude is the real murderer of his father.

_____2. According to Claudius, Prince Fortinbras of Norway is demanding the return of territory that Norway lost to Denmark years earlier because

  A. Denmark is still in mourning for King Hamlet.
  B. Fortinbras believes Denmark is politically unstable as a result of King Hamlet's death.
  C. Denmark is rejoicing for Claudius and Gertrude's marriage.
  D. Hamlet promised it to him.
  E. The present King of Norway is too old to ask.

_____3. In the following speech from Act I, what observation does Claudius make about Hamlet's mourning the death of his father?

~

But you must know, your father lost a father;
That father lost, lost his; and the survivor bound
In filial obligation for some term
To do obsequious sorrow; but to persever
In obstinate condolement, is a course
Of impious stubbornness, 'tis unmanly grief;

~

A. Princes shouldn't mourn the deaths of their fathers.
B. Your father lost a father and so have you.
C. Only Gertrude is entitled to grieve for the death of King Hamlet.
D. Claudius shares Hamlet's grief.
E. It is unmanly for Princes to grieve for too long because they become kings only upon the deaths of their father.

_____ 4. What observation does Ophelia make to her brother Laertes in the following speech before he departs for France?

ᕃᕔ

I shall the effect of this good lesson keep
As watchman to my heart. But good my brother,
Do not as some ungracious pastors do,
Show me the steep and thorny way to heaven,
Whiles like a puffed and reckless libertine
Himself the primrose path of dalliance treads,
And recks not his own rede.

ᕃᕔ

A. That she will stay away from Hamlet.
B. That she will agree to marry Hamlet as soon as he asks.
C. That she will take Laertes' advice only if he promises to enter the priesthood.
D. That she will take his advice, but he needs to take it himself, too.
E. That Laertes' advice is too difficult for her to take right now.

_____ 5. Hamlet swears Horatio and the others to secrecy because

A. Hamlet may need to act strangely in the future.
B. the ghost told him to.
C. Hamlet has sold his soul to the devil.
D. Claudius is guilty.
E. Gertrude is unfaithful.

Postreading Activity
for
Hamlet
Small Group Discussion to Check Comprehension
Act I

Directions: After you've read all of Act I, discuss each of the following questions briefly in small groups. Use the space below each question to note points you may wish to share later. If you need more room, use the back of the page.

1. Why does Horatio feel that Hamlet should be wary of the ghost?

2. What argument does Claudius use to try to comfort Hamlet over the death of his father?

3. What advice does Laertes give to Ophelia about Hamlet?

4. Why does Ophelia agree to the promise about Hamlet with Polonius?

5. Why does Hamlet extract an oath from Horatio and the others about the ghost?

Postreading Activity
for
Hamlet
Critical Thinking Questions
Act I

Directions: To help you develop your understanding of Act I, as your teacher directs you, take time to think about and discuss the following questions. The first question is the focus question, and is the point of the discussion. Don't be concerned that you may not be able to answer this question at first. Proceed to the exploration questions and then return to the focus question.

Focus Question. If you were Hamlet, why would you need to prove the truth of the ghost's story before taking revenge upon Claudius?

Exploration Questions.

1. How do you think you'd react to your mother's remarrying within a few months after the death or divorce of your father?

2. How does the story that the ghost tells contribute to Hamlet's moodiness over the death of his father and the remarriage of his mother?

3. In other works of literature, how have parents and children set up rivalries against each other?

4. If you were Hamlet, how might the ghost's story help you accept the death of your father and the remarriage of your mother?

5. In what other works of literature have characters suddenly lost a parent through death or divorce?

6. How have ghosts or other supernatural events been used as omens of the future in other works of literature?

Postreading Activity
for
Hamlet
Language Exploration
Figurative Language: Simile and Metaphor
Act I

As other poets and playwrights do, Shakespeare also explores such abstract ideas as revenge, personal honor, and the sacrificing of personal goals for public ones in his plays. He often connects abstract ideas with concrete examples through *figurative language*. Although we rarely mean figurative language in a literal sense, it does help us express our ideas more vividly. Two common literary devices associated with figurative language are *simile* and *metaphor*.

A *simile* compares two different terms using <u>like</u> or <u>as</u>. In daily speech we often use similes like these:

&

Sam is <u>as hungry as a bear</u>.
Angel runs <u>like the wind</u>

&

Similarly, Polonius uses simile in giving his advice to Laertes in *Hamlet* (Act I, scene iii),

&

This above all, to thine own self be true,
And <u>it must follow, as the night the day</u>,
Thou canst not then be false to any man.

&

Here, Polonius demonstrates that the logical consequence of being true to oneself is being true to others. The simile points out the logical sequence of Polonius' conclusion by comparing it to the natural sequence of day and night.

Another way to compare two different terms is to use a *metaphor*. Unlike a simile, a metaphor makes a comparison directly without using <u>like</u> or <u>as</u>. As metaphors, the previous examples look like this:

© 1994 by The Center for Applied Research in Education

❧

Sam is a real bear when he's hungry.
Angel breezed across the finish line.

❧

Hamlet uses a metaphor as he promises the ghost of his father to seek revenge upon Claudius (Act I, scene v),

❧

And thy commandment all alone shall live
Within the book and volume of my brain;

❧

The metaphor here compares Hamlet's memory of his vow to the ghost to a clearly defined section (book) within a bound volume.

Directions: The following passages contain examples of simile and metaphor. Working in pairs, small groups, or as your teacher directs, identify the comparisons and then review each passage within the context of the play to develop an interpretation of the passage. You may want to review the quotations within the fuller context of a particular speech.

1. Horatio referring to the ghost's sudden disappearance (Act I, scene i):

❧

And then it started like a guilty thing
Upon a fearful summons.

❧

2. Horatio referring to the rooster's crow (Act I, scene i):

❧

The cock, that is the trumpet of the morn,

❧

3. Claudius referring to King Hamlet's death (Act I, scene ii):

59

❧

Though yet of Hamlet our dear brother's death
The memory be green.

❧

4. Claudius addressing Hamlet's melancholy (Act I, scene ii):

❧

How is it that the clouds still hang on you?

❧

5. Hamlet contemplating life and death (Act I, scene ii):

❧

O that this too too solid flesh would melt,
Thaw and resolve itself into a dew

❧

6. Hamlet continuing to contemplate mortal life (Act I, scene ii):

❧

How weary, stale, flat, and unprofitable
Seem to me the uses of the world!
Fie on't, ah fie, 'tis an unweeded garden
That grows to seed, things rank and gross in nature
Possess it merely.

❧

7. Hamlet commenting upon Gertrude's grief (Act I, scene ii):

❧

. . . she followed my poor father's body,
Like Niobe all tears . . .

❧

8. Horatio telling Hamlet about seeing the ghost (Act I, scene ii):

❧

The apparition comes. I knew your father;
These hands are not more like.

❧

9. Ophelia promising to heed Laertes' advice (Act I, scene iii):

❧

I shall the effect of this good lesson keep
As watchman of my heart.

❧

10. Ophelia requesting Laertes heed his own advice:

❧

But good my brother,
Do not as some good pastors do,
Show me the steep and thorny way to heaven,
Whiles like a puffed and reckless libertine
Himself the primrose path of dalliance treads

❧

Postreading Activity
for
Hamlet
Vocabulary in Context
Act I

Directions: In each of the passages below you will find one of the words from the prereading vocabulary list for Act I. Review the definitions given in the prereading vocabulary. Working individually, in pairs, or in small groups as your teacher directs, examine each of the underlined words in the following passages from Act I. For each word, find the appropriate meaning and develop a brief interpretation of the passage using the play's context.

1. Horatio commenting on the ghost of Hamlet's father (scene i):

   ❧

   It harrows me with fear and wonder.

   ❧

2. Horatio recalling King Hamlet's defeat of King Fortinbras of Norway (scene i):

   ❧

   our last King,
   Whose image even but now appeared to us,
   Was as you know by Fortinbras of Norway,
   Thereto pricked on by a most emulate pride,
   Dared to combat;

   ❧

© 1994 by The Center for Applied Research in Education

3. Horatio relating the trouble that Prince Fortinbras is stirring up in Norway (scene i):

ॐ

> *Now sir, young Fortinbras*
> *Of unimproved mettle hot and full,*
> *Hath in the skirts of Norway here and there*
> <u>*Sharked*</u> *up a list of lawless resolutes*
> *For food and diet to some enterprise*
> *That hath a stomach in't;*

ॐ

4. Hamlet to Horatio who has seen the ghost of King Hamlet (scene ii):

ॐ

> *I pray you all,*
> *If you have hitherto concealed this sight,*
> *Let it be* <u>*tenable*</u> *in your silence still;*

ॐ

5. Laertes to Ophelia, as he prepares to leave for France (scene iii):

ॐ

> *My* <u>*necessaries*</u> *are embarked. Farewell.*

ॐ

6. Laertes advising Ophelia about Hamlet's loving her (scene iii):

ঙ

Then weigh what loss your honor may sustain,
If with too <u>credent</u> ear you list his songs,
Or lose your heart, or your chaste treasure open
To his unmastered importunity.

ঙ

7. Polonius advising Laertes (scene iii):

ঙ

Neither a borrower nor a lender be,
For loan oft loses both itself and friend,
And borrowing dulleth the edge of <u>husbandry</u>.

ঙ

© 1994 by The Center for Applied Research in Education

8. Hamlet commenting upon the weather as he waits on the battlements (scene iv):

ঙ

The air bites <u>shrewdly</u>, it is very cold.

ঙ

9. Horatio agreeing with Hamlet about the weather (scene iv):

ða

It is a nipping and an <u>eager</u> air.

ða

10. Hamlet addressing the ghost of his father (scene iv):

ða

Let me not burst in ignorance, but tell
Why thy canonized bones, <u>hearsed</u> in death,
Have burst their cerements;

ða

Vocabulary Review Quiz
for
Hamlet
Act I

Directions: For each of the italicized words in the sentences below, determine which letter best reflects the use of the word in this context. Place the letter corresponding to your answer in the space to the left of the item number.

____1. When Horatio states that seeing the ghost *harrows* him, he means the situation

A. disturbs him   B. doesn't scare him   C. breaks him up   D. frightens him   E. makes him alert

____2. When Horatio describes King Fortinbras as having *emulate* pride, he suggests that the former King of Norway was

A. stupid   B. ambitious   C. spiteful   D. vengeful   E. greedy

____3. When Horatio states that Prince Fortinbras has *sharked* up an army, he suggests that the Prince of Norway is

A. predatory   B. fool hearty   C. spiteful   D. vengeful   E. silly

____4. When Hamlet asks Horatio and the others for their silence about the ghost to remain *tenable*, Hamlet is asking them to

A. tell only their very close friends   B. sell the information to one of Claudius' informants   C. continue to keep it a secret   D. forget about it   E. pray for the soul of his dead father

____5. For Laertes, his *necessaries* are his

A. necessary belongings   B. his indulgences   C. his inheritance
D. his schoolbooks   E. his military equipment

____6. When Laertes states that Ophelia is too *credent* he means she is

A. too careful about others   B. too thrifty   C. too concerned with her reputation   D. too sincere with Hamlet   E. too eager to believe others

____7. When Polonius cautions his son about *husbandry* he means

A. management of Laertes' time   B. management of Laertes' money
C. management of Reynaldo's household accounts   D. management of Ophelia's inheritance   E. taking care of the family's livestock

_____8. When Hamlet states that "the air bites *shrewdly*," he suggests it is

A. extremely hot   B. extremely cold   C. extremely still   D. extremely spooky   E. extremely scary

_____9. When Horatio refers to the air as *eager*, he suggests it is

A. painfully cold   B. painfully hot   C. a sign something strange may happen   D. a stormy night   E. a clear, peaceful night

_____10. When Hamlet states that his father was *hearsed* he means his father was

A. exhumed   B. carried off   C. pretending to die   D. crowned with appropriate ceremony   E. entombed

ACT II

Focusing Activities
for
Hamlet
Scenarios for Improvisation
Act II

Directions: Presented below are locations and situations involving characters. As your teacher directs you, but before reading an individual scene, pretend to be one of the characters and act out the situation. Don't worry about speaking like the characters in Shakespeare's plays, just try to imagine how you would react to the situation and use your own language. Your teacher may give you a few minutes to discuss what you would like to do with the other performers. Your teacher will probably ask you to act out your scene for others in the class. When you finish, your teacher may ask your classmates to discuss what they've seen.

scene i. Scene: Polonius' house, the day after Hamlet has seen the ghost and sworn to avenge his father's death.

Characters: Hamlet and Ophelia.

Situation: Hamlet has decided to pretend to be insane, so he can devise a plan. In seeing Ophelia, what might he do or say to convince her that he's insane?

scene ii. Scene: The castle.

Characters: Rosencrantz and Guildenstern, two of Hamlet's longtime friends, and Hamlet.

Situation: Claudius has asked Rosencrantz and Guildenstern to find out the source of Hamlet's strange behavior and then report it to him. Improvise a scene where these two friends meet with Hamlet to try to discover what he's up to. Does he allow them to find out or not?

Focusing Activities
for
Hamlet
Small Group Discussion Questions
Act II

Directions: Before reading scenes in Act II, discuss the questions in small groups. You may want to make notes about your discussion so you can share them with classmates or refer back to them after you've read the scene.

scene i.

    1.   Now that Hamlet has sworn to avenge the murder of his father and decided to pretend to be insane, what do you think he might do to convince Claudius and Gertrude of his insanity?

    2.   What might Hamlet do to convince Ophelia and Polonius of his insanity?

scene ii.

    1.   Based upon what you've seen of Claudius, what do you think he might do to discover the source of Hamlet's melancholy?

    2.   How do you think Hamlet will respond to any sudden changes to life at the royal court, such as surprise visitors, a traveling troupe of actors, or changes in diet?

Focusing Activities
for
Hamlet
Speculation Journal
Act II

Directions: This activity is to help you become involved actively with reading the play by helping you to determine a definite purpose for reading. Before you read these scenes in Act II, take a few minutes to respond in writing to the questions below. Don't worry about correct answers here. Use your own experience, what you know, or what you may have heard about the play to speculate about what you think might happen. After reading a scene, you may find that the characters reacted differently than you thought. Don't worry about these differences; just make note of them because you will have opportunities to share these differences in other activities.

scene i. Now that Hamlet has decided to pretend to be mad, so he can develop a plan to avenge his father's murder, what do you think he might do to convince Claudius, Gertrude, Ophelia, and Polonius that he's mad?

scene ii. Based upon what you know about Claudius, what do you think he might do to discover the source of Hamlet's strange behavior?

After Reading Act II: Now that you have finished reading Act II, which of your speculations were most accurate? How do you account for them? Which ones were least like the action of the play? Why do you think you speculated as you did?

Prereading Activity
for
Hamlet
Vocabulary
Act II

Directions: Shakespeare uses the following words in Act II. The section below provides a brief definition of each word and provides a sentence to illustrate its meaning. You may wish to review the words for a particular scene immediately before reading it.

scene i

1. **particular:** (adj.) individual, private or personal gain or interest.
   Example: King Claudius murdered his brother Hamlet to serve a *particular* benefit: he wanted to marry Gertrude.

2. **forgery:** (n.) a lie or deception; a falsehood.
   Example: After hearing Jan tell the story about the big fish that got away again, we suspected the tale was a *forgery*.

3. **conse-quence:** (n.) sequence or succession; the end result of a logical sequence.
   Example: Closing the sale was the logical *consequence* of the effective sales presentation.

4. **unbrace:** (v.) to loosen, untie; to free from restrictive clothing or armor.
   Example: During the twentieth century, women have *unbraced* themselves not only from restrictive clothing styles but also from attitudes that limit their opportunities.

5. **perusal:** (n.) survey; careful study or analysis.
   Example: Before the architect could begin designing the house, she made a careful *perusal* of the site and the family's needs.

scene ii

6. **remedy:** (n.) means to provide relief from evil or wrongdoing; relief or redress.
   Example: Lifelong learning is our *remedy* to lifelong ignorance.

7. **distemper:** (n.) mental or physical illness, disorder, ailment.
   Example: Heavy doses of antibiotics cured the child's *distemper*, which was caused by the infection.

8. **arras:** (n.) a wall tapestry.
   Example: The women spent more than a year weaving the intricate scene into the *arras* that would cover the wall in the reception hall.

9. **fish-monger:** (n.) a fish merchant.
   Example: Our local supermarket has both a butcher and a *fishmonger*.

10. **harp:** (v.) to dwell on excessively.
    Example: Casey's parents *harped* on her about cleaning her room.

Prereading Activity
for
Hamlet
Plot Summaries
Act II

Directions: To help you better understand and follow Hamlet, read the summary of a specific scene before you begin to read it. If you get lost during the scene, you can refer to the summary.

Act II, scene i Some weeks later at Polonius' house, Polonius sends money to Laertes by way of Reynaldo. Polonius instructs Reynaldo first to inquire about Laertes' behavior and to manage Laertes' life, so that Laertes will follow his father's advice before meeting with him.

Ophelia enters, quite upset from a recent meeting with Hamlet. With his clothes in disarray, a silent Hamlet had caught Ophelia by the wrist, held her close, and then at arm's length. He stared at her, sighed deeply, and then left.

Polonius suggests they tell the king about it. He believes Hamlet is mad from frustrated love. Polonius asks Ophelia whether she has met with Hamlet. She replies that she has neither accepted Hamlet's letters nor spoken with him since Polonius told her not to. Polonius interprets this as evidence that his explanation for Hamlet's sudden madness is correct.

Act II, scene ii Claudius has summoned Rosencrantz and Guildenstern, two of Hamlet's college friends, to get them to pump Hamlet and discover the cause of his strange behavior.

Polonius enters and informs the king that the ambassadors have returned from Norway. He then reveals that he will expose the cause of Hamlet's insanity after the ambassadors have given their reports.

Gertrude believes that the death of King Hamlet and her remarriage is the cause.

The ambassadors reveal that Fortinbras' plot against the Danes was stopped.

Polonius explains that Hamlet's madness comes from Ophelia's rejection of him. To prove his theory, Polonius suggests that the king and queen and Polonius watch Hamlet from behind a tapestry when Ophelia goes to him. The king and queen exit.

©1994 by The Center for Applied Research in Education

Hamlet enters, feigning madness, insults Polonius (calling him an old fool) while encouraging Polonius to continue believing that Hamlet's love for Ophelia is the cause of his madness.

Once Polonius is gone, Rosencrantz and Guildenstern enter. Hamlet quickly sees through their pretense and recognizes that his uncle has sent for them. They believe Hamlet is insane, so he encourages this belief.

The troupe of traveling players arrive and recite a story of the death of a king and his queen's grief. Hamlet compares the actor's imagined grief to his own real grief that paralyzes him and prevents him from acting. Hamlet then reveals his own plan for trapping the king into revealing himself: Hamlet will have the actors perform a play that imitates the murder of his father. By watching the king's face, Hamlet will know whether Claudius is guilty or not. Hamlet reveals that this plan is necessary just in case the ghost was an evil spirit who might trick Hamlet into murdering an innocent person. Hamlet would then be damned for all eternity.

Class Period:

CHARACTER ASSIGNMENTS FOR ORAL READING GROUPS
Hamlet

Session 3: Act II, scenes i, ii

Characters	*Group 1*	*Group 2*	*Group 3*	*Group 4*
Polonius	_____	_____	_____	_____
Reynaldo, Cornelius	_____	_____	_____	_____
Ophelia, First Player	_____	_____	_____	_____
Claudius	_____	_____	_____	_____
Gertrude	_____	_____	_____	_____
Rosencrantz	_____	_____	_____	_____
Guildenstern	_____	_____	_____	_____
Voltemand, Hamlet	_____	_____	_____	_____

NAME:_____   DATE:_____

During-reading Activity
for
Hamlet
Character Diary 3
Act II, scenes i and ii

Directions: Use the space below to record your character's reactions to the events of the two scenes in Act II of *Hamlet*. Remember to include a summary of events, explain how your character learned of them, and give your character's reactions to them. If you need additional room, use the back of this sheet.

The Personal Diary of

_____

(character's name)

Six to eight weeks following Act I

_____

_____

_____

_____

_____

_____

_____

_____

_____

_____

_____

_____

_____

_____

_____

_____

_____

During-reading Activity
for
Hamlet
Viewing Act II, scene ii
Claudius Recruits Rosencrantz and Guildenstern
and Hamlet Confronts Them

Directions: After you've read this scene, viewing a film or video version may help you better understand how the text translates into the characters' actions. Although you may want to keep your copy of the play handy, don't be surprised if the actors' script varies from yours. Film scripts often delete or reorder the lines in the play. You may want to note questions you'll need to ask your teacher afterwards. After viewing the scene, take a few minutes to respond to the questions below.

1. Based upon what you've seen, why do you think Rosencrantz and Guildenstern agree to help Claudius?

2. Based upon what you've seen, how do Claudius and Gertrude regard Polonius' explanations about what is causing Hamlet's strange behavior?

3. What enables Hamlet to see Rosencrantz and Guildenstern's motives?

©1994 by The Center for Applied Research in Education

During-reading Activity
for
Hamlet
Guide to Character Development: Hamlet
Act II

Shakespeare reveals his characters in four ways:

᛫ through what the characters say to other characters in dialogue;

᛫ through what the characters reveal about their thoughts through long speeches to the audience called *soliloquies*;

᛫ through what other characters say about them;

᛫ through what they do, their actions.

As you read the play, examine the following scenes for what they reveal about Hamlet's character and fill in the chart briefly using your own words. If you need more room, use the back of the page.

Scene	*What Hamlet says, does, or what others say about him*	*What this reveals about Hamlet's character*
Act II, scene II Polonius meets Hamlet		
Act II, scene ii The arrival of Rosencrantz and Guildenstern		
Act II, scene ii The traveling players arrive		
Act II, scene ii Hamlet's soliloquy ("Ay so God buy to you. Now I am alone.")		

During-reading Activity
for
Hamlet
Guide to Character Development: Gertrude
Act II

Shakespeare reveals his characters in four ways:

❧ through what the characters say to other characters in dialogue;

❧ through what the characters reveal about their thoughts through long speeches to the audience called *soliloquies*;

❧ through what other characters say about them;

❧ through what they do, their actions.

As you read the play, examine the following scenes for what they reveal about Gertrude's character and briefly fill in the chart using your own words. If you need more room, use the back of the page.

Scene	*What Gertrude says, does, or what others say about her*	*What this reveals about Gertrude's character*
Act II, scene ii The arrival of Rosencrantz and Guildenstern		
Act II, scene ii Polonius' explanation of Hamlet's strange behavior		

NAME:_____   DATE:_____

During-reading Activity
for
Hamlet
Guide to Character Development: Claudius
Act II

Shakespeare reveals his characters in four ways:

❧ through what the characters say to other characters in dialogue;

❧ through what the characters reveal about their thoughts through long speeches to the audience called *soliloquies*;

❧ through what other characters say about them;

❧ through what they do, their actions.

As you read the play, examine the following scenes for what they reveal about Claudius' character and fill in the chart briefly using your own words. If you need more room, use the back of the page.

Scene	What Claudius does, says, or what others say about him	What this reveals about Claudius' character
Act II, scene ii The arrival of Rosencrantz and Guildenstern		
Act II, scene ii Polonius' explanation of Hamlet's strange behavior		

During-reading Activity
for
Hamlet
Guide to Character Development: Ophelia
Act II

Shakespeare reveals his characters in four ways:

❧ through what the characters say to other characters in dialogue;

❧ through what the characters reveal about their thoughts through long speeches to the audience called *soliloquies*;

❧ through what other characters say about them;

❧ through what they do, their actions.

As you read the play, examine the following scene for what it reveals about Ophelia's character and fill in the chart briefly using your own words. If you need more room, use the back of the page.

Scene	What Ophelia says, does, or what others say about her	What this reveals about Ophelia's character
Act II, scene i Ophelia tells her father that Hamlet visited her		

NAME:_____   DATE:_____

During-reading Activity
for
Hamlet
Guide to Character Development: Polonius
Act II

Shakespeare reveals his characters in four ways:

ꞷ through what the characters say to other characters in dialogue;

ꞷ through what the characters reveal about their thoughts through long speeches to the audience called *soliloquies*;

ꞷ through what other characters say about them;

ꞷ through what they do, their actions.

As you read the play, examine the following scenes for what they reveal about Polonius' character and fill in the chart briefly using your own words. If you need more room, use the back of the page.

Scene	What Polonius says, does, or what others say about him	What this reveals about Polonius' character
Act II, scene i Polonius' instructions to Reynaldo		
Act II, scene i Ophelia tells her father that Hamlet visited her		
Act II, scene ii Polonius' explanation of Hamlet's strange behavior		
Act II, scene ii Polonius meets Hamlet		

©1994 by The Center for Applied Research in Education

NAME:_____   DATE:_____

Postreading Activity
for
Hamlet
Comprehension Check
Act II

Directions: After you've read all of Act II, use the following questions to check how well you've understood what you've read. For each question, select the most appropriate answer from the choices listed below it. Place the letter corresponding to your answer in the space to the left of the item number.

____1.   Why does Ophelia come to see her father about Hamlet?

A. Because Hamlet proposed to her.
B. Because Hamlet wanted to say goodbye before returning to school.
C. Because Hamlet was acting so strangely.
D. Because Hamlet told her about the ghost.
E. Because Hamlet wanted her help to avenge his father's death.

____2.   Why has Claudius sent for Rosencrantz and Guildenstern?

A. To act as spies against Fortinbras, Prince of Norway.
B. To escort Hamlet back to school at Wittenberg.
C. To cheer Hamlet.
D. He hopes to enlist their help to discover why Hamlet is acting so strangely.
E. To take a message to Laertes, for him to return home.

____3.   What does Polonius propose to do regarding Hamlet's behavior in the following lines?

❧

At such a time, I'll loose my daughter to him.
Be you and I behind an arras then;
Mark the encounter, if he love her not,
And be not from his reason fall'n thereon,
Let me be no assistant for a state,
But keep a farm and carters.

❧

©1994 by The Center for Applied Research in Education

A. That Polonius release Ophelia from her vow not to see Hamlet.
B. That Polonius and Claudius eavesdrop on a meeting between Ophelia and Hamlet.
C. That Claudius give Polonius a new job.
D. That Ophelia is the cause of Hamlet's strange behavior.
E. That Ophelia should fall in love with Hamlet.

____4.   What does Hamlet say to Rosencrantz and Guildenstern in the following lines?

ઠત

But let me conjure you, by the rights of our fellowship, by the consonancy of our youth, by the obligation of our ever-preserved love, and by what more dear a better proposer can charge you withal, be even and direct with me, whether you were sent for or no.

ઠત

A. To be direct and honest with him.
B. To assure Hamlet that they are loyal to him.
C. To tell Hamlet why they've come to see him.
D. To tell Hamlet that they will spy on Claudius for him.
E. To convey a proposal to Ophelia.

____5.   Which of the following is *not* a reason for Claudius and Gertrude to agree with Polonius about the source of Hamlet's apparent madness?

A. Because Polonius explains the history of Hamlet and Ophelia's relationship.
B. Because Polonius reads Hamlet's letter to Ophelia.
C. Because Polonius is an honorable man.
D. Because they are willing to accept unrequited love as a source of madness.
E. Because Polonius eavesdropped on a meeting between Ophelia and Hamlet.

Postreading Activity
for
Hamlet
Small Group Discussion Questions to Check Comprehension
Act II

Directions: After you've read all of Act II, discuss each of the following questions briefly in small groups. Use the space below each question to note points you may want to share later. If you need more room, use the back of the page.

1. Why does Ophelia come to see her father after her encounter with Hamlet?

2. According to Polonius, what is the source of Hamlet's strange behavior?

3. Why does Claudius enlist the help of Rosencrantz and Guildenstern?

4. How does Hamlet manage to foil Claudius' use of Rosencrantz and Guildenstern?

5. How does Hamlet plan to make use of the troupe of traveling players?

NAME:_____   DATE:_____

Postreading Activity
for
Hamlet
Critical Thinking Questions
Act II

Directions: To help you develop your understanding of Act II, as your teacher directs you, take time to think about and discuss these questions. The first question is the focus question and is the point of the discussion. Don't be concerned that you may not be able to answer this question at first. Proceed to the exploration questions and then return to the focus question.

Focus Question. If you were Claudius, how might Hamlet's apparent insanity threaten your power as king?

Exploration Questions.

1. What behaviors do parents use to identify that their children are having problems and may need their help in solving?

2. What does Hamlet gain by pretending to be mad?

3. In the modern world, how have the duties and authority of kings and queens changed since Shakespeare's day when Queen Elizabeth I and King James I ruled England?

4. As a king, why do you think Claudius needs to find the source and remedy of Hamlet's strange behavior?

5. How would insanity affect the duties and authority of a modern monarch?

6. As parents, why is it important for Gertrude and Claudius to know the source of Hamlet's behavior?

Postreading Activity
for
Hamlet
Language Exploration
Figurative Language: Personification and Apostrophe
Act II

We have seen how Shakespeare uses *simile* and *metaphor* to develop figurative language. Like Shakespeare, we also use other devices to express abstract ideas more concretely, such as *personification* and *apostrophe*.

We use *personification* to give human characteristics to inanimate or nonhuman things. We may say that "Love is blind," or argue with the soft drink machine that "eats" our change. In the play, Hamlet addresses his schoolmates Rosencrantz and Guildenstern using a personification of fortune as a woman:

&

What have you, my good friends, deserved at the hands of Fortune,
that she sends you to prison hither?

&

Another figurative device is to address a person or abstract idea directly although it is not or cannot be present. This device is called *apostrophe*. The following expressions are examples:

&

Death, be not proud.

&

or

&

Twinkle, twinkle little star,
How I wonder what you are?

&

At the end of *Hamlet*, Fortinbras surveys the devastation, addressing death directly as though it were human:

©1994 by The Center for Applied Research in Education

જ઼

> *O proud Death,*
> *What feast is toward in thine eternal cell,*
> *That thou so many princes at a shot*
> *So bloodily hast struck?*

જ઼

Directions: The following passages contain examples of personification and apostrophe. Working in pairs, small groups, or as your teacher directs, review each passage within the context of the play and develop an interpretation of the passage. You may want to review the quotations within the fuller context of the particular speech.

1. Horatio referring to the coming dawn (Act I, scene i):

જ઼

> *But look the morn in russet mantle clad*
> *Walks o'er the dew of yon high eastward hill.*

જ઼

2. Claudius responding to Hamlet's decision to remain at court (Act I, scene i):

જ઼

> *This gentle and unforced accord of Hamlet*
> *Sits smiling to my heart*

જ઼

3. Hamlet reflecting upon his mother's remarriage (Act I, scene ii):

જ઼

> *It is not, nor it cannot come to good,*
> *But break, my heart, for I must hold my tongue.*

જ઼

91

4.   Polonius urging Laertes to depart (Act I, scene iii):

❧

The wind sits in the shoulder of your sail,
And you are stayed for.

❧

5.   Polonius advising Laertes (Act I, scene iii):

❧

Give thy thoughts no tongue
Nor any unproportioned thought his act.

❧

6.   Polonius advising Ophelia not to encourage Hamlet's suit (Act I, scene ii):

❧

In few Ophelia,
Do not believe his vows, for they are brokers
Not of that dye which their investments show,
But are implorators of unholy suits,
Breathing like sanctified and pious bonds
The better to beguile.

❧

7. Hamlet responding to the ghost's story (Act I, scene v):

    ❧

    O all you lost of heaven! O earth! What else?
    And shall I couple hell? O fie! Hold, hold, my heart,

    ❧

8. Hamlet swearing to avenge his father's death (Act I, scene v):

    ❧

    So uncle, there you are. Now to my word;
    It is, adieu, adieu, remember me.
    I have sworn't.

    ❧

9. The First Player reciting his speech about Pyrrhus' defeat of Priam
    (Act II, scene ii):

    ❧

    Out, out, thou strumpet Fortune! All you gods,
    In general synod take away her power,
    Break all the spokes and fellies of her wheel,
    And bowl the round knave down the hill of heaven
    As low as fiends

    ❧

10. Hamlet formulating his plan to use the players (Act II, scene ii):

&

> *. . . I have heard*
> *That guilty creatures sitting at play*
> *Have by the cunning of the scene*
> *Been struck so to soul, that presently*
> *They have proclaimed their malefactions.*
> *For murder, though it have no tongue, will speak*
> *With most miraculous organ.*

&

Postreading Activity
for
Hamlet
Vocabulary in Context
Act II

Directions: In each of the passages below you will find one of the words from the prereading vocabulary list for Act II. Review the definitions given in the prereading vocabulary. Working individually, in pairs, or in small groups as your teacher directs, examine each of the underlined words in the following passages from Act II. For each word, use the appropriate meaning and develop a brief interpretation of the passage within the context of the play.

1.   Polonius instructing Reynaldo to find out about Laertes' friends in Paris (scene i):

❧

. . .*and finding* . . .
That they know my son, come you more nearer
Than your <u>particular</u> demands will touch it.

❧

2.   Polonius continuing to instruct Reynaldo (scene i):

❧

. . . *and there put on him*
What <u>forgeries</u> you please, marry none so rank
As may dishonor him, take heed of that;

❧

95

3.   Polonius finishing his instructions to Reynaldo (scene i):

ᴢ

> *. . . be assured*
> *He closes with you in this <u>consequence</u>;*

ᴢ

4.   Ophelia telling Polonius about Hamlet's strange attire (scene i):

ᴢ

> *Lord Hamlet with his doublet all <u>unbraced</u>*
> *. . . he comes before me.*

ᴢ

5.   Ophelia telling Polonius about Hamlet's strange behavior (scene i):

ᴢ

> *He falls to such <u>perusal</u> of my face*
> *As 'a would draw it.*

ᴢ

©1994 by The Center for Applied Research in Education

6. King Claudius instructing Rosencrantz and Guildenstern (scene ii):

ᴣᴥ

> *. . .to gather,*
> *So much as from occasion you may glean,*
> *Whether aught to us unknown afflicts him thus*
> *That opened lies within our <u>remedy</u>.*

ᴣᴥ

7. Claudius to Gertrude (scene ii):

ᴣᴥ

> *He tells me, my dear Gertrude, he hath found*
> *The head and source of all your son's <u>distemper</u>.*

ᴣᴥ

8. Polonius to Claudius and Gertrude (scene ii):

ᴣᴥ

> *At such a time, I'll loose my daughter to him.*
> *Be you and I behind an <u>arras</u> then;*

ᴣᴥ

9.   Hamlet in reply to Polonius' question (scene ii):

૨ક

Excellent well, you are a <u>fishmonger</u>.

૨ક

10.   Polonius reflecting upon Hamlet's concern for Ophelia (scene ii):

૨ક

How say you by that? Still <u>harping</u> on my daughter.

૨ક

©1994 by The Center for Applied Research in Education

NAME:_____   DATE:_____

Vocabulary Review Quiz
for
Hamlet
Act II

Directions: For each of the italicized words in the sentences below, determine which letter best reflects the use of the word in this context. Place the letter corresponding to your answer in the space to the left of the item number.

____1. When Polonius refers to Reynaldo's *particular* demands, he means
A. Polonius' specific requests B. strange demands C. unusual behavior
D. personal business E. secret oath

____2. When Polonius encourages Reynaldo to put *forgeries* upon Laertes character, he means
A. put Laertes in chains and bring him home B. tell "white lies" about Laertes C. exaggerate about Laertes' exploits, destroying his reputation
D. sign Laertes' accounts for him E. make Laertes appear saintly

____3. As Polonius instructs Reynaldo to close in *consequence*, he means
A. reach a logical end B. reach a specifically correct answer C. reach the specific destination of a journey D. do something silly E. express anger and outrage

____4. Ophelia describes Hamlet's clothing as *unbraced*; by this she means
A. fashionable B. dirty C. unlaced D. stained E. rigid

____5. When Hamlet *perused* Ophelia's face, he
A. slapped her B. smeared mud on it C. glanced at it D. held it
E. studied it intently

____6. Claudius and Gertrude want to know whether the cause of Hamlet's madness lies within their *remedy*; therefore, they hope to
A. imprison Hamlet B. make him well C. make him human D. make him their heir E. keep him quiet

____7. When Claudius refers to Hamlet's *distemper*, the King means Hamlet's
A. lively sense of humor B. constant crying C. devotion to his father
D. apparent madness E. desire for revenge

99

____8.   When Polonius hides behind the *arras*, he hides

A. beneath the stairs B. beside the garden gate C. under the bed
D. behind a door E. behind a tapestry

____9.   When Hamlet called Polonius a *fishmonger*, the Prince insulted the old man by calling him

A. a mason B. a field hand C. a fish seller D. a fisherman E. a thief

____10. Hamlet seems to *harp* on Ophelia; therefore, Hamlet is

A. mildly concerned for her B. bored with her C. obsessed with her
D. superior to her E. singing songs about her

ACT III

Focusing Activities
for
Hamlet
Scenarios for Improvisation
Act III

©1994 by The Center for Applied Research in Education

Directions: Presented below are locations and situations involving characters. As your teacher directs you, but before reading an individual scene, pretend to be one of the characters and act out the situation. Don't worry about speaking like the characters in Shakespeare's plays, just try to imagine how you would react to the situation and use your own language. Your teacher may give you a few minutes to discuss what you would like to do with the other performers. Your teacher will probably ask you to act out your scene for others in the class. When you finish, your teacher may ask your classmates to discuss what they've seen.

scene i.   *Scene:* Claudius' chambers.

Characters: Claudius, Rosencrantz, and Guildenstern.

Situation: Improvise a scene where Rosencrantz and Guildenstern report that they have failed to discover the source of Hamlet's strange behavior.

Scene: A public part of the castle.

Characters: Hamlet, Ophelia, Claudius, and Polonius.

Situation: Polonius, who is convinced that Hamlet's strange behavior stems from his thwarted love of Ophelia, wants Claudius to observe how Hamlet responds when he meets Ophelia, whom Polonius has ordered to return all letters and love tokens to Hamlet. Improvise the scene between Hamlet and Ophelia while Claudius and Polonius eavesdrop in the shadows.

scene ii.   *Scene:* The Great Hall of the castle.

Characters: Player King Hamlet, Player Queen Gertrude, and Player King Claudius.

Situation: Improvise the "dumb show" or pantomime that Hamlet has the traveling players perform that he hopes will show proof that Claudius indeed murdered King Hamlet.

scene iv.   *Scene:* Gertrude's chambers, immediately following Claudius' dismissal of the players.

Characters: Gertrude and Hamlet.

Situation: Improvise the scene where Gertrude confronts Hamlet about his offending Claudius and informs him that neither she nor Claudius will tolerate any more of his strange behavior.

Focusing Activities
for
Hamlet
Small Group Discussion Questions
Act III

Directions: Before reading the scenes in Act III, discuss the following questions in small groups. You may want to make notes about your discussion so you can share them with classmates, or refer back to them after you've read the scene.

scene i.

1. When Rosencrantz and Guildenstern report to Claudius that they have failed to discover the source of Hamlet's strange behavior, what might Claudius do next?

2. Polonius believes that Hamlet's behavior comes from his thwarted love for Ophelia. What might Polonius do to prove his theory to Claudius and Gertrude?

scene ii. How might Hamlet alter the plot of "The Murder of Gonzago" to trick Claudius into revealing himself as the murderer of King Hamlet?

scene iii. What do you think Claudius will do to Hamlet after being humiliated publicly by Hamlet's revision of the play?

scene iv. If Gertrude and Hamlet were to meet in private, what would you expect them to say to each other?

Focusing Activities
for
Hamlet
Speculation Journal
Act III

Directions: This activity will help you become actively involved with reading the play by helping you to determine a definite purpose for reading. Before you read these scenes in Act III, take a few minutes to respond in writing to questions below. Don't worry about correct answers here. Use your own experience or what you have read in the play to speculate what you think will happen. After reading a scene you may find that the characters reacted differently than you thought. Don't worry about these differences; just make note of them because you will have opportunities to share these differences in other activities.

scene i. Although Rosencrantz and Guildenstern fail to learn the source of Hamlet's strange behavior, what do you expect them to report to Claudius?

scene ii. How do you think Hamlet has instructed the players to alter "The Murder of Gonzago" so it will trick Claudius into revealing himself as the murderer of King Hamlet?

scene iii. Immediately after Claudius dismisses the play, what do you suppose he will do to Hamlet for humiliating him publicly and threatening his position as king?

©1994 by The Center for Applied Research in Education

scene iv.   Claudius tells Gertrude that he will no longer tolerate Hamlet's strange behavior. When Gertrude summons Hamlet to her chambers, what does she tell him and how does he respond?

After Reading Act III: Now that you have finished reading Act III, which of your speculations were most accurate? How do you account for them? Which ones were least like the action of the play? Why do you think you speculated as you did?

Prereading Activity
for
Hamlet
Vocabulary
Act III

Directions: Shakespeare uses the following words in Act III. The section below provides a brief definition of each word and provides a sentence to illustrate its meaning. You may want to review the words for a particular scene immediately before reading it.

Definitions.

scene i

1. **affront:** (v.) to meet intentionally; confront.
   Example: Jason and his friends only seemed to *affront* the girls in the mall casually; in reality, they had been waiting for several hours.

2. **visage:** (n.) face; assumed appearance; outward appearance.
   Example: Although Steve had just lost his job, he put on the *visage* of self-confidence.

3. **consummation:** (n.) completion; fulfillment; accomplishment, end.
   Example: Although it took six years of part-time studies, graduating with honors was the *consummation* of all of Kathleen's hard work.

4. **coil:** (n.) noisy disturbance; bustle, fuss, trouble; bustle of mortal life.
   Example: After the French team won the international soccer tournament, the *coil* of excited fans soon filled the streets of Paris.

5. **orison:** (n.) prayer, especially a personal one.
   Example: Sister Mary Margarita encouraged her students to remember the homeless in their nightly *orisons*.

6. **calumny:** (n) false charge; intentional damage to another's reputation.
   Example: Because the employee was jealous of the supervisor's success, the employee spread *calumny* about the reasons for it.

©1994 by The Center for Applied Research in Education

scene ii

7. **occulted:** (adj.) hidden.
   Example: My uncle's *occulted* artistic talents didn't bloom until he began to paint seriously after he had retired.

8. **confound:** (v.) to defeat; to overthrow.
   Example: The little boy's desires *confounded* his appetite when he ordered the banana split.

scene iv

9. **mandate:** (n.) command, order, injunction.
   Example: The student knew she was in trouble when the principal's *mandate* to report to the office came over the intercom.

10. **marshal:** (v.) guide; to lead 'as a harbinger.
    Example: In recent years, it has become more common for both parents to *marshal* the bride to the altar.

Prereading Activity
for
Hamlet
Plot Summaries
Act III

Directions: To help you better understand and follow Hamlet, read the summary of a specific scene before you begin to read it. If you get lost during the scene, you can refer to the summary.

Act III, scene i

In the palace, Rosencrantz and Guildenstern report to Claudius and Gertrude that they didn't learn the cause of Hamlet's madness. All Hamlet would tell them was that he felt distracted. Although he spoke freely, Hamlet didn't answer their questions. They also mention that Hamlet did seem pleased to learn of the traveling players. Polonius confirms this and forwards Hamlet's request that the king and queen attend the performance that evening.

Claudius agrees and dismisses Gertrude after informing her that he and Polonius have planned to spy on an arranged meeting between Hamlet and Ophelia. By eavesdropping, they hope to learn whether the cause of Hamlet's madness is his frustrated love for Ophelia.

Polonius directs Ophelia to walk about as if reading a book to distract her from loneliness. He and Claudius hide.

Hamlet, believing himself alone, contemplates his problems. He explores several issues. Is it better to suffer silently or take revenge and risk being killed? Dying would end the sufferings. If death's a sleep, do we dream? And of what? Who would bear the punishments of time, the wrongs of oppressors, the contempt of proud men, the unrequited love, legal delays, the impertinence of officials, and the patience of the just if he can only settle his accounts with such a weapon as a small dagger or hairpin? Who would bear the bundles, if the promise of a life after death didn't make us continue with our problems rather than take on unknown problems after we die? He concludes that his conscience and ability to reason keep him from either killing himself or taking other actions, like killing Claudius now.

When he speaks to Ophelia, she tells him that she wishes to return his love letters because he has rejected her. At first he belittles what he said about her beauty and honesty, but then he admits he loved her once. He then chastises her for believing that he loved her.

Hamlet suggests that Ophelia should enter a nunnery rather than marry a sinner like him. Although he seems innocent enough, he feels it would have been better had he not been born, for he is proud, vengeful, ambitious, and has committed unmentionable sins. Why should he be allowed to live?

Hamlet interrupts himself long enough to call Polonius a fool. He then advises Ophelia if she marries to be uninvolved emotionally. Better to enter a convent. If she marries, it should be to a fool rather than a wise man.

He continues his attack upon Ophelia and women in general. They're two-faced, for they only pretend to be helpless. He blames his love for her for making him mad.

Ophelia concludes that her father is right. Hamlet is quite mad and his words have been attempts to trick her rather than declare his love for her.

Claudius and Polonius enter. Claudius believes Hamlet isn't mad but only troubled and may become dangerous. He decides to send Hamlet to England to retrieve some unpaid tribute. The new sights should distract and remedy Hamlet's behavior.

Polonius agrees with Claudius' plan but still believes Hamlet suffers from unrequited love. Polonius suggests that Gertrude talk with Hamlet after the play. If she can't discover the cause of his madness, then Claudius should send him to England.

Act III, scene ii

Hamlet meets with the traveling players and gives them advice about performing: Speak the lines lightly and with modest gestures. Don't destroy the play by overacting. Don't be overly timid either; use action and word in moderation to complement each other. The true purpose of the play is to mirror human nature. Overacting is ludicrous; it makes the simple person laugh, but it can't make a thinking person grieve. Hamlet then cites examples of actors who have overacted and seemed to be only subhuman creatures attempting to be human. Hamlet also encourages the actors to stick to the script rather than improvise for their own vanity. He then urges them to go rehearse.

Polonius, Rosencrantz, and Guildenstern ask whether the players are ready. Hamlet sends all to urge the actors to prepare.

He spots Horatio, and after praising Horatio's honor and trustworthiness, Hamlet tells him about how the play will imitate King Hamlet's murder. Hamlet asks Horatio to watch Claudius' face. If the king shows guilt, then they will know that the ghost indeed was Hamlet's father and not some evil spirit. They agree to meet afterwards to compare what they saw.

The royal court enters. Hamlet refuses to sit with his mother, choosing instead to sit at Ophelia's feet and lay his head in her lap.

The play begins. The actors first pantomime the king's murder as the ghost described it. Ophelia asks what the pantomime means. The actors then proceed to speak the lines and act out the full play. After the

111

actor king and queen have established their long-standing marriage and love for each other, Hamlet asks the king and queen how they like the play. Pretending to know the play, Hamlet explains that it depicts a murder in Vienna. When the actor representing Claudius poisons the king, Claudius rises and stops the play, clearing the hall.

Hamlet and Horatio meet. They agree that Claudius' reaction proves his guilt and they now believe the ghost to be King Hamlet's.

Guildenstern tells Hamlet that King Claudius is angry, but Gertrude wishes to speak with him. Hamlet agrees to go.

When Guildenstern again tries to get Hamlet to reveal the source of his madness, Hamlet replies it is ambition. As Hamlet jests with Guildenstern, Polonius comes to summon Hamlet to the queen. Hamlet replies that he will come soon.

Left alone, Hamlet realizes that now, at midnight, he could take revenge upon Claudius and Gertrude more easily. Instead, he plans to speak to his mother harshly although he still loves her.

Act III, scene iii

Claudius decides to send Rosencrantz and Guildenstern to England with Hamlet. Rosencrantz and Guildenstern promise to protect Hamlet, for, as heir to the throne, they recognize that his death would have political consequences.

Polonius promises to listen from behind the tapestry as Hamlet meets with Gertrude.

Left alone, Claudius reveals his guilt. He murdered his brother. His guilt is so strong that it prevents him praying for forgiveness. The deed is done. What good would prayer do? Could forgiveness benefit him when he still has the crown, his ambition, and Gertrude, his reasons for murdering his brother? In life, the wicked often win out over the just. In heaven, however, the truth wins out. He knows he should repent but cannot. He recognizes that he's damned unless he repents. He calls upon angels to help him and begins to pray.

Hamlet sees Claudius praying and considers killing him. However, Hamlet decides that killing Claudius while he prayed might cause Claudius to go to heaven. Instead, Hamlet decides to wait until Claudius has no hope of redemption and then kill him. Hamlet leaves. As Claudius finishes, he comments that his thoughts were on life while he prayed, so the prayers didn't work. Ironically, Hamlet has missed a chance to avenge his father's murder.

Act III, scene iv

In Gertrude's chamber, Polonius urges the queen to tell Hamlet that his behavior has been unbearable and that only her intervention has protected him. Polonius then hides behind the tapestry.

©1994 by The Center for Applied Research in Education

Gertrude points out that Hamlet has offended his (step)father. Hamlet turns her words to the truth: She has offended King Hamlet, his father. When Gertrude reminds him that she is the queen, he reminds her that she is her husband's brother's wife now. Outraged and fearing for her safety, she calls for help. When Polonius also calls for help, Hamlet thinks Claudius is behind the tapestry, and stabs him.

Hamlet tells Gertrude the truth. Referring to the heroic figures in the tapestry, he tells her that Claudius killed King Hamlet. He asks for a reason because he cannot accept passion as Gertrude and Claudius' motivation. They are too old. Instead, he asks what devil possessed her.

Gertrude stops Hamlet, seeing the truth. Hamlet continues to attack Claudius. His father's ghost enters and urges Hamlet to pursue revenge.

Because Gertrude can't see the ghost, she believes Hamlet's talking to the air confirms his madness. When Hamlet explains, she insists the ghost is an hallucination.

Rather than dwell upon his supposed madness, Hamlet urges Gertrude to repent. He urges her not to go to Claudius that night. Each time she can refuse will make it easier not to go the next time.

When she's ready to confess, he promises to receive her.

Finally, Hamlet extracts a promise from Gertrude. She won't let Claudius seduce her and learn that Hamlet has faked his madness. Hamlet then leaves for England, suspecting that Claudius may have ordered Rosencrantz and Guildenstern to kill him.

Class Period:

CHARACTER ASSIGNMENTS FOR ORAL READING GROUPS
Hamlet

Session 4: Act III, scenes i, ii

Characters	_Group 1_	_Group 2_	_Group 3_	_Group 4_
Claudius	___	___	___	___
Rosencrantz, Horatio	___	___	___	___
Guildenstern, Lucianius	___	___	___	___
Ophelia	___	___	___	___
Polonius	___	___	___	___
Hamlet	___	___	___	___
First Player, Player King	___	___	___	___
Chorus, Player Queen	___	___	___	___

114

Class Period:

CHARACTER ASSIGNMENTS FOR ORAL READING GROUPS
Hamlet

Session 5: Act III, scenes iii, iv

Characters	*Group 1*	*Group 2*	*Group 3*	*Group 4*
Claudius	_____	_____	_____	_____
Guildenstern	_____	_____	_____	_____
Rosencrantz	_____	_____	_____	_____
Polonius	_____	_____	_____	_____
Hamlet (scene iii)	_____	_____	_____	_____
Gertrude	_____	_____	_____	_____
Hamlet (scene iv)	_____	_____	_____	_____
Ghost	_____	_____	_____	_____

During-reading Activity
for
Hamlet
Character Diary 4
Act III, scenes i and ii

Directions: Use the space below to record your character's reactions to the events of the first two scenes in Act III of *Hamlet*. Remember to include a summary of events, explain how your character learned of them, and give your character's reactions to them. Because this act has four scenes, you may want to record your character's entries as you read each scene. If you need additional room, use the back of this sheet.

The Personal Diary of

_____
(character's name)

The next day

_____

_____

_____

_____

_____

_____

That evening

_____

_____

_____

_____

_____

_____

During-reading Activity
for
Hamlet
Character Diary 5
Act III, scenes iii and iv

Directions: Use the space below to record your character's reactions to the events of the last two scenes in Act III of *Hamlet*. Remember to include a summary of events, explain how your character learned of them, and give your character's reactions to them. Because this act has four scenes, you may want to record your character's entries as you read each scene. If you need additional room, use the back of this sheet.

The Personal Diary of

_____
(character's name)

Later that evening

_____

_____

_____

_____

_____

_____

_____

_____

_____

_____

_____

_____

_____

_____

During-reading Activity
for
Hamlet
Viewing Act III, scene ii
Claudius and the Royal Court Watch the Traveling Players

Directions: After you've read this scene, viewing a film or video version may help you better understand how the text translates into the characters' actions. Although you may want to keep your copy of the play handy, don't be surprised if the actors' script varies from yours. Film scripts often delete or reorder the lines in the play. You many want to note questions you need to ask your teacher afterwards. After viewing the scene, take a few minutes to respond to the questions below.

1. Based upon what you've seen, how do Hamlet's language and actions change as he speaks first to the players, then to Horatio, and finally as a member of the audience watching the play?

2. How does the director use the camera to show Claudius' reaction to the play and how either Hamlet or Horatio respond to it?

3. When Hamlet once more confronts Rosencrantz and Guildenstern at the end of the scene, in what ways has his distrust of them changed?

During-reading Activity
for
Hamlet
Guide to Character Development: Hamlet
Act III

Shakespeare reveals his characters in four ways:

- through what the characters say to other characters in dialogue;

- through what the characters reveal about their thoughts through long speeches to the audience called *soliloquies*;

- through what other characters say about them;

- through what they do, their actions.

As you read the play, examine the following scenes for what they reveal about Hamlet's character and fill in the chart briefly using your own words. If you need more room, use the back of the page.

Scene	What Hamlet says, does, or what others say about him	What this reveals about Hamlet's character
Act III, scene i Hamlet meets Ophelia		
Act III, scene ii Hamlet instructs the Players		
Act III, scene ii Hamlet confides in Horatio		
Act III, scene ii The Players perform		
Act III, scene ii Claudius ends the play		

Act III, scene ii Hamlet meets again with Rosencrantz and Guildenstern		
Act III, scene iii Hamlet encounters Claudius praying		
Act III, scene iv Hamlet confronts his mother		

NAME:________________________________ DATE:________________

During-reading Activity
for
Hamlet
Guide to Character Development: Gertrude
Act III

Shakespeare reveals his characters in four ways:

- through what the characters say to other characters in dialogue;
- through what the characters reveal about their thoughts through long speeches to the audience called *soliloquies*;
- through what other characters say about them;
- through what they do, their actions.

As you read the play, examine the following scenes for what they reveal about Gertrude's character and fill in the chart briefly using your own words. If you need more room, use the back of the page.

Scene	*What Gertrude says, does, or what others say about her*	*What this reveals about Gertrude's character*
Act III, scene ii The Players perform		
Act III, scene ii Claudius ends the play		
Act III, scene iv Hamlet confronts his mother		

©1994 by The Center for Applied Research in Education

During-reading Activity
for
Hamlet
Guide to Character Development: Claudius
Act III

Shakespeare reveals his characters in four ways:

- through what the characters say to other characters in dialogue;

- through what the characters reveal about their thoughts through long speeches to the audience called *soliloquies*;

- through what other characters say about them;

- through what they do, their actions.

As you read the play, examine the following scenes for what they reveal about Claudius' character and fill in the chart briefly using your own words. If you need more room, use the back of the page.

Scene	*What Claudius says, does, or what others say about him*	*What this reveals about Claudius' character*
Act III, scene i Rosencrantz and Guildenstern report to Claudius		
Act III, scene i Hamlet meets Ophelia		
Act III, scene ii The Players perform		
Act III, scene iii Rosencrantz and Guildenstern again report to Claudius		

Act III, scene iii Claudius' soliloquy ("O my of- fence is rank, it smells to heaven . . .")		

**During-reading Activity
for
*Hamlet***
Guide to Character Development: Horatio
Act III

Shakespeare reveals his characters in four ways:

🍂 through what the characters say to other characters in dialogue;

🍂 through what the characters reveal about their thoughts through long speeches to the audience called *soliloquies*;

🍂 through what other characters say about them;

🍂 through what they do, their actions.

As you read the play, examine the following scenes for what they reveal about Horatio's character and fill in the chart briefly using your own words. If you need more room, use the back of the page.

Scene	*What Horatio says, does, or what others say about him*	*What this reveals about Horatio's character*
Act III, scene i Hamlet confides in Horatio		
Act III, scene ii The Players perform		
Act III, scene ii Claudius ends the play		

124

During-reading Activity
for
Hamlet
Guide to Character Development: Ophelia
Act III

Shakespeare reveals his characters in four ways:

❧ through what the characters say to other characters in dialogue;

❧ through what the characters reveal about their thoughts through long speeches to the audience called *soliloquies*;

❧ through what other characters say about them;

❧ through what they do, their actions.

As you read the play, examine the following scenes for what they reveal about Ophelia's character and fill in the chart briefly using your own words. If you need more room, use the back of the page.

Scene	What Ophelia says, does, or what others say about her	What this reveals about Ophelia's character
Act III, scene i Hamlet meets Ophelia		
Act III, scene ii The Players perform		

During-reading Activity
for
Hamlet
Guide to Character Development: Polonius
Act III

Shakespeare reveals his characters in four ways:

🙣 through what the characters say to other characters in dialogue;

🙣 through what the characters reveal about their thoughts through long speeches to the audience called *soliloquies*;

🙣 through what other characters say about them;

🙣 through what they do, their actions.

As you read the play, examine the following scenes for what they reveal about Polonius' character and fill in the chart briefly using your own words. If you need more room, use the back of the page.

Scene	What Polonius says, does, or what others say about him	What this reveals about Polonius' character
Act III, scene i Hamlet meets Ophelia		
Act III, scene ii The Players perform		
Act III, scene iv Hamlet confronts his mother		

©1994 by The Center for Applied Research in Education

Postreading Activity
for
Hamlet
Comprehension Check
Act III

Directions: After you've read all of Act III, use the following questions to check how well you've understood what you've read. For each question, select the most appropriate answer from the choices listed below it. Place the letter corresponding to your answer in the space to the left of the item number.

____1. Hamlet has the traveling players revise one of their scripts so it

A. is much shorter than it would have been otherwise.
B. recreates the murder of Hamlet's father.
C. recreates the marriage of Claudius and Gertrude.
D. retells the last battle King Hamlet fought.
E. allows Hamlet to propose to Ophelia.

____2. Although Hamlet gets an opportunity to kill Claudius, why doesn't he?

A. Because he knows that Claudius is innocent.
B. Because Hamlet is convinced that Claudius is guilty because he ended the play suddenly.
C. Because killing Claudius while he's praying will send him to heaven.
D. Because he plans to poison Claudius later.
E. Because Hamlet is convinced that the ghost lied.

____3. Which pair of opposites does Hamlet contemplate in the following lines?

&

To be, or not to be, that is the question—
Whether 'tis nobler in the mind to suffer
The slings and arrows of outrageous fortune,
Or to take arms against a sea of troubles,
And by opposing end them.

&

    A. Whether Ophelia loves him or not.

    B. Whether dreams occur to the dead who seem to sleep.

    C. Whether Claudius is guilty or innocent, based upon the evidence.

    D. Whether to suffer the injustices of life passively or to seek to redress them actively.

    E. Whether love and death are the same.

___4.   What does Claudius reveal in the following lines?

❦

O my offence is rank, it smells to heaven;
It hath the primal eldest curse upon't,
A brother's murder. Pray can I not,
Though inclination be as sharp as will,
My stronger guilt defeats my strong intent,
And like a man to double business bound,
I stand in pause where I shall first begin,
And both neglect.

❦

    A. That he is guilty of his brother's murder and will ask forgiveness.

    B. That he is guilty of killing his brother but cannot pray for forgiveness.

    C. That he will pray for forgiveness for killing his brother and marrying Gertrude.

    D. That no sin is so great that it can't be forgiven.

    E. That he is guilty of neglecting his family.

___5.   Why does Hamlet kill Polonius?

    A. He believes it is Claudius hiding behind the arras.

    B. He hates the old man for interfering in his relationship with Ophelia.

    C. He meant to kill Gertrude who was crying out for help.

    D. He's driven to seek revenge by the ghost.

    E. He thought Polonius was attacking him.

Postreading Activity
for
Hamlet
Small Group Discussion to Check Comprehension
Act III

Directions: After you've read all of Act III, discuss each of the following questions briefly in small groups. Use the space below each question to note points you may want to share later. If you need more room, use the back of the page.

1. How do Polonius and Claudius plan to discover the source of Hamlet's strange behavior?

2. What do Polonius and Claudius believe they have learned from their plan?

3. What leads Hamlet to believe that Claudius has revealed himself to be the murderer of King Hamlet?

4. Why does Hamlet fail to kill Claudius when he has the chance?

5. What promise does Gertrude make to Hamlet when they are alone in her chambers?

Postreading Activity
for
Hamlet
Critical Thinking Questions
Act III

Directions: To help you develop your understanding of Act III, as your teacher directs you, take time to think about and discuss these questions. The first question is the focus question and is the point of the discussion. Don't be concerned that you may not be able to answer this question at first. Proceed to the exploration questions and then return to the focus question.

Focus Question. What would make you as willing as Hamlet is to accept Claudius' reaction to the play as sufficient proof of his guilt?

Exploration Questions.

1. From your experience, how can you tell when someone is guilty without having definite proof?

2. Why does Hamlet believe that altering "The Murder of Gonzago" will provide proof of Claudius' guilt?

3. In a modern court, what kinds of evidence are necessary to convict a murderer?

4. What signs of guilt is Hamlet willing to accept as sufficient proof of Claudius' guilt?

5. Why would it be difficult to find sufficient evidence to convict Claudius of his brother's murder in a modern court?

6. How have characters in other works of literature relied more on their instincts than evidence to establish guilt or innocence?

Postreading Activity
for
Hamlet
Language Exploration
Symbol
Act III

When we use a word, object, or image to represent another idea or concept, it becomes a *symbol*. For example, the American flag is a symbol of our country and its democratic form of government. Another example would be when people drive luxury automobiles or wear expensive watches as symbols to show that they have enough wealth to afford these items.

In literature, too, authors often use symbols. For example, in Act I, scene i, Marcellus explains the symbolic importance of the ghost disappearing once the rooster crows:

❧

It faded on the crowing of the cock.
Some say that ever 'gainst that season comes
Wherein our Saviour's birth is celebrated
This bird of dawning singeth all night long,
And then they say no spirit dare stir abroad;
The nights are wholesome, then no planets strike,
No fairy takes, nor witch hath power to charm,
So hallowed and so gracious is that time.

❧

Here, the rooster's crow symbolizes not just the coming of daylight but also the time when spirits, the motions of the planets, fairies, and witches have no power.

Directions: The following lines contain symbols. Working in pairs, small groups, or as your teacher directs, review each passage in the context of the play and decide what each symbol suggests to the reader.

1. Hamlet contemplating his mother's remarriage (Act I, scene ii):

❧

. . . frailty, thy name is woman.

❧

2. Hamlet commenting on the quick marriage of Claudius and Gertrude (Act I, scene ii):

*Thrift, thrift, Horatio. The funeral baked meats
Did coldly furnish forth the marriage tables.*

3. Hamlet addressing the ghost (Act I, scene iv):

*. . . why the sepulchre,
Wherein we saw thee quietly interred
Hath oped his ponderous and marble jaws
To cast thee up again.*

4. The ghost telling about his death (Act I, scene iv):

*Thus was I sleeping by a brother's hand
Of life, of crown, of Queen, at once dispatched.*

5. Polonius replying to Claudius (Act II, scene ii):

❧

Give first admittance to th' ambassadors;
My news shall be the fruit to that great feast.

❧

6. Hamlet pondering life and death (Act III, scene i):

❧

To be or not to be, that is the question—
Whether 'tis nobler in the mind to suffer
The slings and arrows of outrageous fortune,

❧

7. Hamlet pondering life and death (Act III, scene i):

❧

To die, to sleep—
To sleep, perchance to dream,

❧

8. Hamlet reflecting upon the nature of death (Act III, scene i):

ॐ

But that the dread of something after death,
The undiscovered country, from whose bourn
No traveler returns . . .

ॐ

9. Hamlet expressing his sincere admiration of Horatio's honesty (Act III, scene ii):

ॐ

No, let the candied tongue lick absurd pomp

ॐ

10. Claudius reflecting upon his murder of his brother and his desire for absolution (Act III, scene iii):

ॐ

Bow stubborn knees, and heart with strings of steel
Be soft as sinews of the new-born babe.

ॐ

NAME:_____   DATE:_____

Postreading Activity
for
Hamlet
Vocabulary in Context
Act III

Directions: In each of the passages below you will find one of the words from the prereading vocabulary list for Act III. Review the definitions given in the prereading vocabulary. Working individually, in pairs, or in small groups as your teacher directs, examine each of the underlined words in the following passages from Act III. For each word, use the appropriate meaning and develop a brief interpretation of the passage within the context of the play.

1. Claudius revealing his plan to eavesdrop on Hamlet and Ophelia (scene i):

    ❧

    Sweet Gertrude leave us too
    For we have closely sent for Hamlet hither,
    That he, as 'twere by accident, may here
    Affront Ophelia.

    ❧

2. Polonius to Ophelia (scene i):

    ❧

    'Tis too much proved, that with devotion's <u>visage</u>
    And pious action we do sugar o'er
    The devil himself.

    ❧

3.   Hamlet contemplating the meaning of life and death (scene i):

ะ

> *To die, to sleep—*
> *No more; and by a sleep to say we end*
> *The heart-ache, and the thousand natural shocks*
> *That flesh is heir to; 'tis a <u>consummation</u>*
> *Devoutly to be wished.*

ะ

4.   Hamlet contemplating the meaning of life and death (scene i):

ะ

> *For in that sleep of death what dreams may come*
> *When we have shuffled off this mortal <u>coil</u>.*

ะ

©1994 by The Center for Applied Research in Education

5.   Hamlet, addressing Ophelia (scene i):

ะ

> *Soft you now,*
> *The fair Ophelia.—Nymph, in thy <u>orisons</u>*
> *Be all my sins remembered.*

ะ

6.   Hamlet to Ophelia (scene i):

ﮗ

If thou dost marry, I'll thee this plague for thy dowry—be thou as chaste as ice, as pure as snow, thou shalt not escape calumny.

ﮗ

7.   Hamlet to Horatio (scene ii):

ﮗ

Observe my uncle. If his <u>occulted</u> guilt
Do not itself unkennel in one speech,
It is a damned ghost that we have seen,

ﮗ

8.   Player Queen to Player King (scene ii):

ﮗ

O <u>confound</u> the rest,
Such love must needs be treason in my breast.

ﮗ

9.   Hamlet to Gertrude (scene iv):

ès

There's letters sealed, and my two school fellows,
Whom I will trust as I will adders fanged,
They bear the <u>mandate</u>;

ès

10.   Hamlet to Gertrude (scene iv):

ès

. . . they must sweep my way,
And marshal me to <u>knavery</u>.

ès

Vocabulary Review Quiz
for
Hamlet
Act III

Directions: For each of the italicized words in the sentences below, determine which letter best reflects the use of the word in this context. Place the letter corresponding to your answer in the space to the left of the item number.

____1. When Claudius and Polonius decide that Ophelia will *affront* Hamlet, they mean she will

A. meet Hamlet completely by accident.
B. confront Hamlet angrily.
C. meet Hamlet intentionally.
D. retreat from Hamlet.
E. accompany Hamlet to England.

____2. When Polonius suggests to Ophelia not to trust the *visage* of devotion, he's suggesting that

A. the actions of devotion aren't trustworthy.
B. the devotion may be an hallucination.
C. the words don't have any meaning.
D. the outward appearance of devotion isn't trustworthy.
E. the devotion is outdated.

____3. Hamlet sees death as a *consummation* to life's problems; therefore,

A. death is only the beginning of a better life for Hamlet.
B. death is only an end to life.
C. death interrupts life.
D. death extends life.
E. death is the logical end to life and its problems.

____4. Shakespeare invented the expression *mortal coil*. It refers to

A. the bustle of daily living.
B. the boredom of daily living.
C. the unpleasantness of life.
D. the eternal problems of living.
E. the routine nature of death.

___5. When Hamlet asks Ophelia about her *orisons*, he

   A. asks her forgiveness.
   B. asks to be remembered in her prayers.
   C. asks to be forgotten.
   D. asks to be mentioned in her next letter to Laertes.
   E. asks to be avenged.

___6. When Hamlet mentions *calumny* to Ophelia, he

   A. suggests that she's in danger.
   B. hopes she will forgive him and agree to marry him.
   C. suggests that someone will damage her reputation intentionally.
   D. hopes she'll avoid him in the future.
   E. suggests she should forget about marriage to anyone.

___7. As Hamlet uses *occulted*, he means

   A. satanic.
   B. mysterious.
   C. magical.
   D. spiritual.
   E. hidden.

___8. To *confound* means to

   A. overthrow.
   B. confuse.
   C. conform.
   D. refuse.
   E. surrender.

___9. Claudius issues a *mandate* to have Hamlet killed once he gets to England. Here, mandate means

   A. a majority.
   B. a recall.
   C. official order.
   D. a demand.
   E. an official reward or bounty.

©1994 by The Center for Applied Research in Education

___10. When Hamlet states that Rosencrantz and Guildenstern *marshal* him to knavery, he

A. is ordering them to fight for him.
B. suggests they're ushering him towards danger.
C. is suggesting that Claudius has bribed them.
D. fears that he will have to turn against his friends.
E. suggests that Gertrude order their deaths.

ACT IV

Focusing Activities
for
Hamlet
Scenarios for Improvisation
Act IV

Directions: Presented below are locations and situations involving characters. As your teacher directs you, but before reading an individual scene, pretend to be one of the characters and act out the situation. Don't worry about speaking like the characters in Shakespeare's plays, just try to imagine how you would react to the situation and use your own language. Your teacher may give you a few minutes to discuss what you would like to do with the other performers. Your teacher will probably ask you to act out your scene for others in the class. When you finish, your teacher may ask your classmates to discuss what they've seen.

scene i. *Scene:* Claudius' chambers.

Characters: Gertrude and Claudius.

Situation: Improvise the scene where Gertrude tells Claudius that Hamlet has killed Polonius accidentally. What does Claudius do in response?

scenes ii and iii. *Scene:* The castle.

Characters: Rosencrantz and Guildenstern, Hamlet, Claudius.

Situation: Improvise the scene where Claudius sends Rosencrantz and Guildenstern to Hamlet to recover the body of Polonius. What does Hamlet tell them and what do they report to Claudius afterwards?

scene v. *Scene:* The castle.

Characters: Claudius, Gertrude, Laertes, and Ophelia.

Situation: Because Ophelia has suffered the separation from her brother, the loss of Hamlet's love, and the death of her father at Hamlet's hand, Ophelia loses touch with reality. Improvise the scene where Ophelia demonstrates true madness to Gertrude, Claudius, and Laertes.

scene vii. *Scene:* The castle.

Characters: Claudius and Laertes.

Situation: Laertes seeks to avenge his father's death. Claudius wishes to be rid of Hamlet. What sort of plan might they make to get rid of Hamlet?

Focusing Activities
for
Hamlet
Small Group Discussion Questions
Act IV

Directions: Before reading the scenes in Act IV, discuss the following questions in small groups. You may wish to make notes about your discussion, so you can share it with classmates or refer back to it after you've read the scene.

scene i.   Based upon what you know about Claudius, how do you expect him to react to the news that Hamlet has killed Polonius?

scene ii.   Because Hamlet continues to pretend to be mad, how might he respond to Rosencrantz and Guildenstern's request for Polonius' body?

scene iii.   When Rosencrantz and Guildenstern fail to recover Polonius' body, what do you think Claudius might do to secure his position as King and still punish Hamlet?

scene iv.   How do you think Hamlet will feel about himself as a prince and as an avenger of his father's murder if he were to encounter Prince Fortinbras of Norway, who is leading an army against the Poles?

scene v.   How do you think Ophelia might respond to the death of her father after being separated from her brother Laertes and losing Hamlet's love?

scenes vi and vii. Laertes wants to avenge his father's death. Claudius, in order to retain his throne, has sent Hamlet to England with orders for the English to kill him. If Hamlet were to return suddenly, what might Claudius and Laertes do to take revenge on Hamlet?

Focusing Activities
for
Hamlet
Speculation Journal
Act IV

Directions: This activity is to help you become involved actively with reading the play by helping you to determine a definite purpose for reading. Before you read these scenes in Act IV, take a few minutes to respond in writing to the questions below. Don't worry about correct answers here. Use your own experience, what you know, or what you may have heard about the play to speculate about what you think might happen. After reading a scene, you may find that the characters reacted differently than you thought. Don't worry about these differences; just make note of them because you will have opportunities to share these differences in other activities.

scene i. How do you suppose Claudius will respond to learning that Hamlet has killed Polonius?

scene ii. What would Hamlet have to gain by continuing to pretend to be mad when Rosencrantz and Guildenstern come to request the body of Polonius?

scene iii. How might Hamlet's response to the request for Polonius' body differ if it came from Claudius?

scene iv. Compare Fortinbras' role as prince and heir to the throne of Norway to Hamlet's.

©1994 by The Center for Applied Research in Education

scene v. Based upon what you've seen of Ophelia, how do you suppose she might react to the news of her father's death after being separated from her brother and losing Hamlet's love?

scenes vi and vii. Claudius has sent Hamlet to England with a letter ordering the English to kill him. Laertes wants revenge upon Hamlet for killing his father. How might Claudius use Laertes to secure his throne?

After Reading Act IV: Now that you have finished reading Act IV, which of your speculations were most accurate? How do you account for them? Which ones were least like the action of the play? Why do you think you speculated as you did?

Prereading Activity
for
Hamlet
Vocabulary
Act IV

Directions: Shakespeare uses the following words in Act IV. The section below provides a brief definition of each word and provides a sentence to illustrate its meaning. You may want to review the words for a particular scene immediately before reading it.

Definitions.

scene i

1. **contend:** (v.) struggle; oppose.
   Example: Although Enid *contended* an incumbent, she won the election on the issues.

2. **providence:** (n.) foresight, guardianship.
   Example: After the birth of my nephew, my sister and brother-in-law would only trust the *providence* of my mother to keep their son safe when they had to be out of town overnight.

scene ii

3. **knavish:** (adj.) dishonest; like a knave, rascal, or rogue.
   Example: In our culture, we expect used car salespersons to behave *knavishly*.

scene iii

4. **multitude:** (n.) crowd, mob, throng.
   Example: To the dismay of the bodyguards, the skillful politician waded into the crowd gathered at the airport after she spoke to the *multitude*.

5. **appliance:** (n.) medicine; means; services
   Example: Mustard plasters were once common *appliances* for relieving the congestion of a chest cold.

scene iv

6. **convey-**
   ance: (n.) channel, way, passage.
   Example: The causeway was the only *conveyance* from the island to the mainland.

scene v

7. **beggar:** (n.) to make a beggar of; impoverish; exhaust means.
   Example: Because the teenager had *beggared* all his resources to buy the used car, he had to ask his parents for a loan to pay to repair it.

8. **rabble:** (n.) mob, angry crowd
   Example: The *rabble* stormed the palace and deposed the monarch.

9. **commune:** (v.) share; communicate verbally.
   Example: When I was a teenager, I used to go to a flat rock beside the river to *commune* with nature and write poetry.

10. **obscure:** (adj.) hidden, without prominence.
    Example: Until Robert Waller wrote *The Bridges of Madison County,* Winterset was an *obscure* little town in Iowa.

Prereading Activity
for
Hamlet
Plot Summaries
Act IV

Directions: To help you better understand and follow Shakespeare's play, read the summary of specific scenes immediately before you begin to read the original. If you get lost during the scene, refer to the summary again.

Act IV, scene i

Shortly after Gertrude and Claudius meet with Rosencrantz and Guildenstern, Gertrude asks to speak to Claudius alone. She tells him that Hamlet is indeed mad and that her son has killed Polonius accidentally and taken the body away. Claudius, believing Hamlet's madness makes the prince dangerous, decides to send Hamlet away immediately. He then calls Rosencrantz and Guildenstern. The King tells them what Hamlet has done and asks them to find Hamlet and bring Polonius' body to the chapel.

Act IV, scene ii

When Rosencrantz and Guildenstern find Hamlet, the Prince will not tell them where Polonius' body is, only that he has buried it. As Hamlet continues to be mad, he compares Rosencrantz and Guildenstern to sponges who spy for the King, who wrings information from them and sends them off again.

Act IV, scene iii

Claudius has called Hamlet before the court. When Hamlet comes, he uses his act to remind Claudius that kings, like beggars, are mortal. Claudius then sends Hamlet to England.

Act IV, scene iv

As Hamlet goes to the ship, he meets the Captain of Fortinbras' army. The captain informs Hamlet that the Norwegian army needs to cross Denmark to attack Poland. The Norwegians plan the attack to take a disputed, but worthless piece of land.

Alone, Hamlet contemplates his own inability to act as a brave prince should. First Hamlet points out that the ability to reason separates humankind from beasts. Hamlet then berates himself for not taking action, though he has had sufficient provocation: the Norwegian army, his father's murder, Gertrude's marriage.

Act IV, scene v

Gertrude agrees to see Ophelia, who has become quite insane as a result of her unrequited love for Hamlet as well as her father's death and hasty burial. After Claudius witnesses Ophelia's madness, he sends Horatio and other gentlemen to keep an eye on her.

Claudius then reveals that Laertes, Ophelia's brother, has returned from France secretly. Laertes bursts into court, vowing to avenge his father's death.

Claudius meets Laertes bravely and calms him down, convincing him that the king wasn't responsible for Polonius' death. When Ophelia returns, her madness again upsets Laertes. He goes out with Claudius.

Act IV, scene vi
A sailor delivers several letters from Hamlet: for Claudius, Gertrude, and Horatio. Horatio reads his and learns that Hamlet was taken prisoner by pirates on the voyage, but they freed him in return for a favor. Hamlet sent Rosencrantz and Guildenstern on to England. Hamlet is returning to Denmark and promises to tell Horatio of his plans.

Act IV, scene vii
Claudius manipulates Laertes skillfully. Claudius has told Laertes that Hamlet killed Polonius. When Laertes asks why Hamlet wasn't punished, Claudius explains that it would have hurt Gertrude too much and that the people love Hamlet too much.

Laertes seeks to avenge his father's death. The messenger delivers Hamlet's letter asking permission to see the king and explain his return.

Claudius turns Laertes' desire for revenge into a plot to murder Hamlet. Because Laertes is a skilled swordsman, he suggests a fencing match which would provide Laertes the opportunity to kill Hamlet. Laertes agrees, but decides to put poison on both his rapier and dagger. To ensure the success of the plot, Claudius agrees to poison Hamlet's wine. Then Gertrude informs them that Ophelia has drowned herself.

Class Period:

CHARACTER ASSIGNMENTS FOR ORAL READING GROUPS
Hamlet

Session 6: Act IV, scenes i, ii, iii, iv

Characters	*Group 1*	*Group 2*	*Group 3*	*Group 4*
Claudius	_____	_____	_____	_____
Gertrude	_____	_____	_____	_____
Rosencrantz	_____	_____	_____	_____
Guildenstern	_____	_____	_____	_____
Hamlet (scene i, ii)	_____	_____	_____	_____
Fortinbras	_____	_____	_____	_____
Captain	_____	_____	_____	_____
Hamlet (scene iii, iv)	_____	_____	_____	_____

154

Class Period:

CHARACTER ASSIGNMENTS FOR ORAL READING GROUPS

Hamlet

Session 7: Act IV, scenes v, vi, vii

Characters	_Group 1_	_Group 2_	_Group 3_	_Group 4_
Gertrude	_____	_____	_____	_____
Gentlemen, Sailor, Messenger	_____	_____	_____	_____
Horatio	_____	_____	_____	_____
Ophelia	_____	_____	_____	_____
Claudius	_____	_____	_____	_____
Laertes	_____	_____	_____	_____
Other Danes	_____	_____	_____	_____
Servant	_____	_____	_____	_____

During-reading Activity
for
Hamlet
Character Diary 6
Act IV, scenes i, ii, iii, iv

Directions: Use the space below to record your character's reactions to the events of the first four scenes in Act IV of Hamlet. Remember to include a summary of events, explain how your character learned of them, and give your character's reactions to them. Because this act has seven scenes, you may wish to record your character's entries as you read each scene. If you need additional room, use the back of this sheet.

The Personal Diary of

_____
(character's name)

Still later, the same evening

_____
_____
_____
_____
_____
_____
_____
_____
_____
_____
_____
_____
_____
_____
_____
_____

During-reading Activity
for
Hamlet
Character Diary 7
Act IV, scenes v, vi, vii

Directions: Use the space below to record your character's reactions to the events of the last three scenes in Act IV of Hamlet. Remember to include a summary of events, explain how your character learned of them, and give your character's reactions to them. Because this act has seven scenes, you may wish to record your character's entries as you read each scene. If you need additional room, use the back of this sheet.

The Personal Diary of
_____
(character's name)

A few weeks following the end of scene iv

_____
_____
_____
_____
_____
_____
_____
_____
_____
_____
_____
_____
_____
_____
_____
_____

During-reading Activity
for
Hamlet
Viewing Act IV, scene v
Ophelia Goes Mad

Directions: After you've read this scene, viewing a film or video version may help you better understand how the text translates into the characters' actions. Although you may want to keep your copy of the play handy, don't be surprised if the actors' script varies from yours. Film scripts often delete or reorder the lines in the play. You many want to note questions you need to ask your teacher afterwards. After viewing the scene, take a few minutes to respond to the questions below.

1. Based upon what you've seen, how do Claudius and Gertrude respond to Ophelia's insanity?

2. How does Laertes respond to Ophelia's insanity?

3. How do the actors' tones of voice, facial expressions, and gestures enhance the meaning of Shakespeare's words?

©1994 by The Center for Applied Research in Education

©1994 by The Center for Applied Research in Education

NAME:_____   DATE:_____

During-reading Activity
for
Hamlet
Guide to Character Development: Hamlet
Act IV

Shakespeare reveals his characters in four ways:

❧ through what the characters say to other characters in dialogue;

❧ through what the characters reveal about their thoughts through long speeches to the audience called *soliloquies*;

❧ through what other characters say about them;

❧ through what they do, their actions.

As you read the play, examine the following scenes for what they reveal about Hamlet's character and fill in the chart briefly using your own words. If you need more room, use the back of the page.

Scene	*What Hamlet says, does, or what others say about him*	*What this reveals about Hamlet's character*
Act IV, scene ii Rosencrantz and Guildenstern attempt to recover Polonius' body		
Act IV, scene iii Claudius attempts to recover Polonius' body		
Act IV, scene iv Hamlet's soliloquy ("How all occasions do inform against me, And spur my dull revenge! . . .")		

During-reading Activity
for
Hamlet
Guide to Character Development: Gertrude
Act IV

Shakespeare reveals his characters in four ways:

🙠 through what the characters say to other characters in dialogue;

🙠 through what the characters reveal about their thoughts through long speeches to the audience called *soliloquies*;

🙠 through what other characters say about them;

🙠 through what they do, their actions.

As you read the play, examine the following scenes for what they reveal about Gertrude's character and fill in the chart briefly using your own words. If you need more room, use the back of the page.

Scene	What Gertrude says, does, or what others say about her	What this reveals about Gertrude's character
Act IV, scene i Gertrude relates Polonius' murder		
Act IV, scene v Ophelia's reaction to the murder of Polonius		
Act IV, scene vii Ophelia's drowning herself		

©1994 by The Center for Applied Research in Education

NAME:_____   DATE:_____

During-reading Activity
for
Hamlet
Guide to Character Development: Claudius
Act IV

Shakespeare reveals his characters in four ways:

- through what the characters say to other characters in dialogue;

- through what the characters reveal about their thoughts through long speeches to the audience called *soliloquies*;

- through what other characters say about them;

- through what they do, their actions.

As you read the play, examine the following scenes for what they reveal about Claudius' character and fill in the chart briefly using your own words. If you need more room, use the back of the page.

Scene	What Claudius says, does, or what others say about him	What this reveals about Claudius' character
Act IV, scene i Gertrude relates Polonius' murder		
Act IV, scene iii Claudius attempts to recover Polonius' body		
Act IV, scene v Ophelia's reaction to the murder of Polonius		

Act IV, scene vii The explanation of Polonius' hasty burial		
Act IV, scene vii Laertes' desire for revenge		

During-reading Activity
for
Hamlet
Guide to Character Development: Horatio
Act IV

Shakespeare reveals his characters in four ways:

✒ through what the characters say to other characters in dialogue;

✒ through what the characters reveal about their thoughts through long speeches to the audience called *soliloquies*;

✒ through what other characters say about them;

✒ through what they do, their actions.

As you read the play, examine the following scenes for what they reveal about Horatio's character and fill in the chart briefly using your own words. If you need more room, use the back of the page.

Scene	What Horatio says, does, or what others say about him	What this reveals about Horatio's character
Act IV, scene v Ophelia's reaction to Polonius' death		
Act IV, scene vi Receipt of Hamlet's letter		

During-reading Activity
for
Hamlet
Guide to Character Development: Laertes
Act IV

Shakespeare reveals his characters in four ways:

❧ through what the characters say to other characters in dialogue;

❧ through what the characters reveal about their thoughts through long speeches to the audience called *soliloquies*;

❧ through what other characters say about them;

❧ through what they do, their actions.

As you read the play, examine the following scenes for what they reveal about Laertes' character and fill in the chart briefly using your own words. If you need more room, use the back of the page.

Scene	What Laertes says, does, or what others say about him	What this reveals about Laertes' character
Act IV, scene v The murder of Polonius		
Act IV, scene v Ophelia's reaction to the murder of Polonius		
Act IV, scene vii The explanation of Polonius' hasty burial		
Act IV, scene vii Ophelia's drowning herself		

During-reading Activity
for
Hamlet
Guide to Character Development: Ophelia
Act IV

Shakespeare reveals his characters in four ways:

• through what the characters say to other characters in dialogue;

• through what the characters reveal about their thoughts through long speeches to the audience called *soliloquies*;

• through what other characters say about them;

• through what they do, their actions.

As you read the play, examine the following scene for what it reveals about Ophelia's character and fill in the chart briefly using your own words. If you need more room, use the back of the page.

Scene	What Ophelia says, does, or what others say about her	What this reveals about Ophelia's character
Act IV, scene v The murder of Polonius		

165

Postreading Activity
for
Hamlet
Comprehension Check
Act IV

Directions: After you've read all of Act IV, use the following questions to check how well you've understood what you've read. For each question, select the most appropriate answer from the choices listed below it. Place the letter corresponding to your answer in the space to the left of the item number.

____1.   Why does Claudius fear being blamed for Hamlet's killing of Polonius?

A. Because Hamlet is under Claudius' guardianship.
B. Because Claudius plotted with Hamlet to kill Polonius.
C. Because Polonius was in Gertrude's chambers.
D. Because Laertes will want to avenge Polonius' murder.
E. Because Claudius is already a known murderer.

____2.   Why does Claudius send Rosencrantz and Guildenstern to meet with Hamlet once again?

A. To find out why Hamlet killed Polonius.
B. To find out whether Hamlet has sent word to Laertes.
C. To recover the body of Polonius.
D. To discover whether Hamlet has eloped with Ophelia.
E. To arrest Hamlet for the murder of Polonius.

____3.   What does Claudius suggest with these lines?

❧

> *And England, if my love thou hold'st at aught—*
> *As my great power thereof may give thee sense,*
> *Since yet thy cicatrice looks raw and red*
> *After the Danish sword, and thy free awe*
> *Pays homage to us—thou mayst not coldly set*
> *Our sovereign process, which imports at full*
> *By letters congruing to that effect*
> *The present death of Hamlet.*

❧

©1994 by The Center for Applied Research in Education

A. That the English will acknowledge Denmark's sovereignty over England.
B. That the English are cowards.
C. That the English will understand his intentions and kill Hamlet.
D. That the English are traitors.
E. That the English will kill Hamlet.

___4. What does Gertrude suggest about Ophelia's actions in the following lines?

ð

She speaks much of her father, says she hears
There's tricks i' th' world, and hems, and beats her heart,
Spurns enviously at straws, speaks things in doubt
That carry but half sense.

ð

A. Ophelia claims to be talking to the ghost of Polonius.
B. Ophelia talks to herself but doesn't make much sense.
C. Ophelia is mourning the death of her father normally.
D. Ophelia pines for the love of Hamlet.
E. Ophelia needs to see her brother.

___5. Which of the following is *not* a reason for Claudius to enlist Laertes in his plot to kill Hamlet?

A. Laertes wishes to avenge his father's murder.
B. Ophelia has committed suicide.
C. Laertes will follow Claudius' commands blindly.
D. Laertes is a skillful swordsman.
E. Laertes is angry that his father was buried hastily.

Postreading Activity
for
Hamlet
Small Group Discussion Questions to Check Comprehension
Act IV

Directions: After you've read all of Act IV, discuss each of the following questions briefly in small groups. Use the space below each question to note points you may want to share later. If you need more room, use the back of the page.

1. Why is Claudius concerned that Hamlet has killed Polonius?

2. When Rosencrantz and Guildenstern come to inquire about Polonius' body, how does Hamlet respond? What do Rosencrantz and Guildenstern believe about Hamlet as a result of the encounter?

3. What does Claudius hope to gain by sending Hamlet to England?

4. What causes Ophelia to drown herself?

5. How does Claudius finally enlist the help of Laertes?

NAME:_____   DATE:_____

Postreading Activity
for
Hamlet
Critical Thinking Questions
Act IV

Directions: To help you develop your understanding of Act IV, as your teacher directs you, take time to think about and discuss these questions. The first question is the focus question and is the point of the discussion. Don't be concerned that you may not be able to answer this question at first. Proceed to the exploration questions and then return to the focus question.

Focus Question.   During much of the play, Hamlet seems either incapable or unwilling to act. What arguments can you find that Hamlet's accidental killing of Polonius is the beginning of his acting decisively?

Exploration Questions.

1.   What distinctions do you make between irrational behavior and insane behavior?

2.   Why does Claudius word his letter to the English so they will understand that they are to kill Hamlet?

3.   Why does society consider insanity a reasonable defense in murder cases?

4.   In what ways is Claudius' decision to send Hamlet to England a rational decision and in what ways is it an impulsive one?

5.   Why might you consider Hamlet's killing of Polonius an accident?

6.   If the play ended with Act IV, scene v, what evidence would a modern jury need to convict Claudius of the murder of Prince Hamlet?

Postreading Activity
for
Hamlet
Language Exploration
Imagery
Act IV

In addition to figurative language, symbolism, and verbal irony, Shakespeare also uses *imagery:* language that appeals to the senses of sight, touch, taste, smell, and hearing. Because our senses provide our direct contact with the world, poets often appeal to these sensory experiences to help convey more abstract ideas. Shakespeare often develops imagery in combination with figurative language.

Notice how Claudius appeals to the senses to reveal his guilt for murdering Hamlet's father (Act III, scene iii):

&

O my offence is rank, it smells to heaven;	*(smell)*
It hath the primal eldest curse upon't,	
A brother's murder. Pray can I not,	
Though inclination be as sharp as will.	*(touch)*
My stronger guilt defeats my strong intent,	
And like a man to double business bound.	*(touch)*
I stand in pause where I shall first begin,	
And both neglect. What if this cursed hand	
Were thicker than itself with brother's blood,	*(touch and sight)*
Is there not rain enough in the sweet heavens	*(sight, taste, touch)*
To wash it white as snow? Whereto serves mercy	*(sight and touch)*
But to confront the visage of offence?	*(sight)*

&

Directions: The following passages from Acts III and IV contain examples of imagery. Working in pairs, small groups, or as your teacher directs, review each passage in the context of the play and decide which sense Shakespeare appeals to and what the passage suggests to the reader.

1. Polonius instructing Ophelia (Act III, scene i)

૨ક

—Read on this book,
That show of such an exercise may colour
Your loneliness.

૨ક

2. Claudius responding to Polonius' instructions (Act III, scene i):

૨ક

How smart a lash that speech doth give my conscience.

૨ક

3. Ophelia returning letters to Hamlet (Act III, scene i):

૨ક

My honoured lord, you know right well you did,
And with them words of so sweet breath composed
As made the things more rich. Their perfume lost,
Take these again, for to the noble mind
Rich gifts wax poor when givers prove unkind.

૨ક

4. Hamlet chastising Ophelia (Act III, scene i):

૨ક

If thou dost marry, I'll give thee this plague for they dowry—be thou
as chaste as ice, as pure as snow, thou shalt not escape calumny.

૨ક

5.   Hamlet advising the players (Act III, scene ii):

        ❧

> *Speak the speech I pray you as I pronounced it to you, trippingly on the tongue; but if you mouth it as many of our players do, I had as lief the town crier spoke my lines.*

        ❧

6.   Claudius addressing Gertrude (Act IV, scene i):

        ❧

> *There's matter in these sighs, these profound heaves.*
> *You must translate, 'tis fit we understand them.*

        ❧

7.   Gertrude commenting upon Hamlet's reaction to killing Polonius (Act IV, scene i):

        ❧

> *To draw apart the body he hath killed,*
> *O'er whom his very madness, like some ore*
> *Among a mineral of metals base,*
> *Shows itself pure; 'a weeps for what is done.*

        ❧

©1994 by The Center for Applied Research in Education

8. Hamlet commenting on the nature of death (Act IV, scene iii):

    ❧

    A man may fish with the worm that hath eat of a king, and eat of the fish that hath fed of that worm.

    ❧

9. Claudius commenting upon Ophelia's madness and Laertes' return (Act IV, scene v):

    ❧

    Last, and as much containing as all these,
    Her brother is in secret come from France,
    Feeds on his wonder, keeps himself in clouds,
    And wants not buzzers to infect his ear
    With pestilent speeches of his father's death,

    ❧

10. Ophelia grieving (Act IV, scene v):

    ❧

    O heat, dry up my brains, tears seven times salt
    Burn out the sense and virtue of mine eyes.

    ❧

Postreading Activity
for
Hamlet
Vocabulary in Context
Act IV

Directions: In each of the passages below you will find one of the words from the prereading vocabulary list for Act IV. Review the definitions given in the prereading vocabulary. Working individually, in pairs, or in small groups as your teacher directs, examine each of the underlined words in the following passages from Act IV. For each word, use the appropriate meaning and develop a brief interpretation of the passage within the context of the play.

1.   Gertrude responds to Claudius when he asks about Prince Hamlet (scene i):

ea

Mad as the sea and wind when both <u>contend</u>
Which is the mightier.

ea

2.   Claudius to Gertrude, upon learning that Hamlet has killed Polonius (scene i):

ea

It will be laid to us, whose <u>providence</u>
Should have kept short, restrained and out of haunt
This mad young man;

ea

©1994 by The Center for Applied Research in Education

3.   Hamlet to Rosencrantz and Guildenstern (scene ii):

ᨃ

I am glad of it; a <u>knavish</u> speech sleeps in a foolish ear.

ᨃ

4.   Claudius discussing Hamlet with his court (scene iii):

ᨃ

How dangerous is it that this man goes loose,
You must not we put the strong law on him.
He is loved by the distracted <u>multitude</u>.

ᨃ

5.   Claudius discussing Hamlet with his court (scene iii):

ᨃ

Diseases desperate grown
By desperate <u>appliance</u> are relieved,
Or not at all.

ᨃ

6.   Fortinbras sending his captain to Claudius (scene iv):

ᨃ

Go captain, from me greet the Danish King:
Tell him, that by his license Fortinbras
Craves the <u>conveyance</u> of a promised march
Over his kingdom.

ᨃ

7. Claudius commenting upon Ophelia's brother, Laertes', return from France (scene v):

ஓ

Her brother is in secret come from France,
Feeds on his wonder, keeps himself in clouds,
And wants not buzzers to infect his ear
With pestilent speeches of his father's death;
Wherein necessity of matter <u>*beggared*</u>,
Will nothing stick our person to arraign
In ear and ear.

ஓ

8. A gentleman informing Claudius of the commotion Laertes is causing outside (scene v):

ஓ

The <u>*rabble*</u> *call him lord,*

. . .

They cry, choose we! Laertes shall be king!

ஓ

9. Claudius to Laertes (scene v):

ஓ

Laertes, I must <u>*commune*</u> *with your grief,*
Or you deny me right.

ஓ

©1994 by The Center for Applied Research in Education

176

10. Laertes commenting upon his father's hasty burial (scene v):

ಶಿ

His means of death, his <u>obscure</u> burial,
No trophy, sword, nor hatchment o'er his bones,
No noble rite, nor formal ostentation,
Cry to be heard as 'twere from heaven to earth,
That I must call't in question.

ಶಿ

Vocabulary Review Quiz
for
Hamlet
Act IV

Directions: For each of the italicized words in the sentences below, determine which letter best reflects the use of the word in this context. Place the letter corresponding to your answer in the space to the left of the item number.

____1.   When Gertrude states that the wind and sea *contend*, she means that

A. a storm has passed.
B. a storm approaches.
C. the elements seem to have made peace with each other.
D. the elements struggle against each other.
E. the elements seem to have offended each other.

____2.   When Claudius refers to Gertrude's and his *providence*, he refers to their

A. stewardship.
B. guardianship.
C. husbandry.
D. insight.
E. authority.

____3.   When Hamlet uses *knavish*, he means that someone is

A. incisive, like a knife.
B. dishonest, like a rogue.
C. cautious, like a cat
D. disturbed, like a maniac.
E. silly, like a jester.

____4.   When Claudius refers to the *multitude*, he means

A. the courtiers.
B. the monks in the nearby abbey.
C. the people.
D. the servants of the royal household.
E. the traveling players.

_____5. As Claudius uses *appliance*, he means

A. an electrical apparatus.
B. medicinal remedy.
C. the one applying for jobs.
D. something added on.
E. something indispensable.

_____6. Fortinbras requests a *conveyance*; therefore, he

A. requests an audience with the King.
B. orders King Claudius to let him pass.
C. insists that Claudius let his army through.
D. challenges Claudius to join forces with him.
E. seeks official permission to march through Denmark.

_____7. As Claudius uses *beggar* it means

A. to beg.
B. to overcome.
C. to improve.
D. to impoverish.
E. to restore.

_____8. The *rabble* who call for Laertes to be King are

A. a revolutionary movement.
B. a band of guerrillas.
C. a mob outside the palace.
D. a gang of outlaws.
E. a community of monks.

_____9. Claudius' request to *commune* is a request to

A. share and communicate verbally.
B. oppose and debate loudly.
C. observe and passively resign.
D. to pray and receive absolution.
E. to oppose and coerce quietly.

_____10. Laertes refers to his father's burial as *obscure* because

A. it was done ostentatiously and elaborately.
B. it was done without appropriate ceremony.
C. it occurred at night.
D. it occurred during a bad storm.
E. it occurred after Laertes' return.

ACT V

Focusing Activities
for
Hamlet
Scenarios for Improvisation
Act V

Directions: Presented below are locations and situations involving characters. As your teacher directs you, but before reading an individual scene, pretend to be one of the characters and act out the situation. Don't worry about speaking like characters in Shakespeare's plays, just try to imagine how you would react to the situation and use your own language. Your teacher may give you a few minutes to discuss what you would like to do with the other performers. Your teacher will probably ask you to act out your scene for others in the class. When you finish, your teacher may ask your classmates to discuss what they've seen.

scene i. *Scene:* A churchyard.

Characters: Hamlet, Claudius, Gertrude, and Laertes.

Situation: Improvise the scene where Hamlet discovers Ophelia's funeral in progress.

scene ii. *Scene:* The castle.

Characters: Hamlet, Laertes, Claudius, and Gertrude.

Situation: Improvise the duel between Hamlet and Laertes, so that you bring the play to a satisfactory conclusion.

Focusing Activities
for
Hamlet
Small Group Discussion Questions
Act V

Directions: Before reading the scenes in Act V, discuss the following questions in small groups. You may want to make notes about your discussion so you can share them with classmates or refer back to them after you've read the scene.

scene i. Based upon what you know about the characters of Hamlet and Laertes, how would you expect each to react to the funeral of Ophelia?

scene ii. If Claudius and Laertes' plan succeeds, Laertes will kill Hamlet with the poisoned sword during the duel. What alternative ending can you construct that would lead to a more satisfying conclusion to the play?

NAME:_____   DATE:_____

Focusing Activities
for
Hamlet
Speculation Journal
Act V

Directions: This activity is to help you become involved actively with reading the play by helping you to determine a definite purpose for reading. Before you read these scenes in Act V, take a few minutes to respond in writing to the questions below. Don't worry about correct answers here. Use your own experience, what you know, or what you may have heard about the play to speculate about what you think might happen. After reading a scene, you may find that the characters reacted differently than you thought. Don't worry about these differences; just make note of them because you will have opportunities to share these differences in other activities.

scene i.

1. If you were Laertes, what might you write in a personal journal upon learning of Ophelia's suicide?

2. If you were Hamlet, what might you write in a personal journal upon learning of Ophelia's suicide?

scene ii. In what ways do you expect the final outcome of the play to be different from Claudius and Laertes' plan to have Laertes kill Hamlet with a poisoned sword during the duel?

After Reading Act V: Now that you have finished reading Act V, which of your speculations were most accurate? How do you account for them? Which ones were least like the action of the play? Why do you think you speculated as you did?

Prereading Activity
for
Hamlet
Vocabulary
Act V

Directions: Shakespeare uses the following words in Act V. The section that follows provides a brief definition of each word and provides a sentence to illustrate its meaning. You may want to review the words for a particular scene immediately before reading it.

Definitions.

scene i.

1. **absolute** (adj.) complete; entire; to fullest degree.
   Example: The parents' concern was *absolute* until the firefighters rescued their children.

2. **fancy** (n.) imagination; fantasy; whimsicality.
   Example: Jim Davis' fertile *fancy* is the source of his comic strip "Garfield."

3. **maimed** (adj.) rendered powerless; incomplete.
   Example: After the lightning shorted our son's Nintendo, he could only stare in disbelief at its *maimed* shell.

4. **quick** (n.) the living; alive; endowed with life.
   Example: It is not for us, the *quick,* to judge the deeds of the dead.

5. **outface** (v.) to outdo, shame, silence.
   Example: The teacher's penetrating stare *outfaced* the unruly students into silence.

scene ii

6. **indis-**
   cretion (n.) unguarded or unwary conduct or behavior.
   Example: When driving on interstate highways, a moment's *indiscretion* can lead to an accident.

7. **scarf** (v.) to clothe, cover, or wrap as in a scarf.
   Example: At the end of the melodrama, once the hero paid the mortgage, the villain *scarfed* his cape around himself and fled.

8. **packet** (n.) intrigue; plot.
   Example: Because Steve had the reputation as a prankster, the principal suspected him immediately as the source of the *packet* to put a frog in the teacher's desk.

9. **angle** (n.) baited fishing hook; trap; deception.
   Example: The unscrupulous salesperson used an unbelievably low price as an *angle* to bring customers into the store.

10. **carriage** (n.) carrier, support.
    Example: Even after battles were fought with rifles, military officers often wore swords and scabbards with elaborate *carriages*.

Prereading Activity
for
Hamlet
Plot Summaries
Act V

Directions: To help you better understand and follow *Hamlet,* read the summary of a specific scene before you begin to read it. If you get lost during the scene, you can refer to the summary.

Act V, scene i

The sexton and the gravedigger prepare Ophelia's grave. They complain that the privileged can have a Christian burial even though they commit suicide. Hamlet and Horatio enter. The gravedigger continues to work, throwing up a skull while he digs. Hamlet uses the skull to reflect upon how death affects human ambition.

Ophelia's funeral interrupts Hamlet. As Laertes speaks of his grief, he jumps into the grave to hold his sister one last time. Hamlet steps forward and speaks of his grief too, joining Laertes in the grave. Hamlet soon realizes that his ranting is as foolish as Laertes.

Act V, scene ii

A short while later, Hamlet tells Horatio of his journey. While at sea, Hamlet read Claudius' letter and destroyed it. He wrote a new letter to the king of England, urging peace, and sealed it with his father's signet. He sent the letter with Rosencrantz and Guildenstern. Hamlet also reveals that the only safe way to deal with Claudius is to suspect the worst from him.

Osric brings Hamlet Claudius' challenge to the fencing match. Because of the greater odds on Hamlet as the less skillful fencer, the King has bet on him heavily. Calmly, Hamlet agrees to the match. Hamlet reasons that if he wins, the king will win; if Hamlet looses, he will only shame himself.

The court arrives for the fencing match. Hamlet first apologizes to Laertes, who accepts this grudgingly.

They fence. Hamlet scores first, claiming one. Claudius tries to get Hamlet to drink the poisoned wine, but he refuses. They fence a second time. Hamlet again scores. Gertrude is so pleased with Hamlet's performance that she drinks a toast with the poisoned wine from his cup.

As they fence for a third time, Laertes wounds a defenseless Hamlet. In the scuffle, they exchange rapiers. Hamlet wounds Laertes.

Gertrude realizes she's drunk poisoned wine and dies. Laertes, now weakened from the poison on his weapons, falls and reveals the plot. Hamlet stabs Claudius and forces him to drink the wine. The king

©1994 by The Center for Applied Research in Education

dies. Before Hamlet dies, he asks Horatio to report the true story to the world. Hamlet also names Fortinbras as his successor.

Fortinbras, returning from Poland, claims the throne and reveals that Hamlet's letter brought peace with England and that Rosencrantz and Guildenstern are dead.

Class Period:

CHARACTER ASSIGNMENTS FOR ORAL READING GROUPS

Hamlet

Session 8: Act V, scene i

Characters	*Group 1*	*Group 2*	*Group 3*	*Group 4*
Sexton				
Gravedigger				
Hamlet				
Horatio				
Laertes				
Claudius				
Gertrude				
Priest				

Class Period:

CHARACTER ASSIGNMENTS FOR ORAL READING GROUPS
Hamlet

Session 9: Act V, scene ii

Characters	*Group 1*	*Group 2*	*Group 3*	*Group 4*
Hamlet	_____	_____	_____	_____
Horatio	_____	_____	_____	_____
Osric	_____	_____	_____	_____
Lord, First Ambassador	_____	_____	_____	_____
Claudius	_____	_____	_____	_____
Gertrude	_____	_____	_____	_____
Laertes	_____	_____	_____	_____
Fortinbras	_____	_____	_____	_____

During-reading Activity
for
Hamlet
Character Diary 8
Act V, scene i

Directions: Use the space below to record your character's reactions to the events of the first scene in Act V of Hamlet. Remember to include a summary of events, explain how your character learned of them, and give your character's reactions to them. Because this act has two scenes, you may want to record your character's entries as you read each scene. If you need additional room, use the back of this sheet.

The Personal Diary of

_____
(character's name)

Four or five days after Act IV

_____

_____

_____

_____

_____

_____

_____

_____

_____

_____

_____

_____

_____

_____

During-reading Activity
for
Hamlet
Character Diary 9
Act V, scene ii

Directions: Use the space below to record your character's reactions to the events of the last scene in Act V of Hamlet. Remember to include a summary of events, explain how your character learned of them, and give your character's reactions to them. Because this act has two scenes, you may want to record your character's entries as you read each scene. If you need additional room, use the back of this sheet.

The Personal Diary of

_____
(character's name)

Later that day

_____
_____
_____
_____
_____
_____
_____
_____
_____
_____
_____
_____
_____
_____
_____
_____
_____
_____
_____

During-reading Activity
for
Hamlet
Viewing Act V, scene ii
Hamlet and Laertes' Duel

Directions: After you've read this scene, viewing a film or video version may help you better understand how the text translates into the characters' actions. Although you may want to keep your copy of the play handy, don't be surprised if the actors' script varies from yours. Film scripts often delete or reorder the lines in the play. You many want to note questions you need to ask your teacher afterwards. After viewing the scene, take a few minutes to respond to the questions below.

1.   What has the director done to let you know as a viewer that Hamlet's wine has been poisoned?

2.   When Hamlet and Laertes scuffle, how do you know that they've managed to exchange weapons?

3.   How do the actors' tones of voice, facial expressions, and gestures enhance the meaning of Shakespeare's words?

©1994 by The Center for Applied Research in Education

NAME:_____   DATE:_____

During-reading Activity
for
Hamlet
Guide to Character Development: Hamlet
Act V

Shakespeare reveals his characters in four ways:

ϫ through what the characters say to other characters in dialogue;

ϫ through what the characters reveal about their thoughts through long speeches to the audience called *soliloquies;*

ϫ through what other characters say about them;

ϫ through what they do, their actions.

As you read the play, examine the following scenes for what they reveal about Hamlet's character and fill in the chart briefly using your own words. If you need more room, use the back of the page.

Scene	What Hamlet says, does, or what others say about him	What this reveals about Hamlet's character
Act V, scene i Hamlet and Horatio encounter the gravedigger and the sexton		
Act V, scene i Ophelia's funeral		
Act V, scene ii Hamlet recounts his adventure at sea and shares his thoughts about Claudius		
Act V, scene ii Osric brings news of the odds on the duel		

Act V, scene ii Hamlet scores the first hit		
Act V, scene ii Hamlet wounds Laertes		
Act V, scene ii Laertes reveals the conspiracy		

NAME:_____   DATE:_____

During-reading Activity
for
Hamlet
Guide to Character Development: Gertrude
Act V

Shakespeare reveals his characters in four ways:

❧ through what the characters say to other characters in dialogue;

❧ through what the characters reveal about their thoughts through long speeches to the audience called *soliloquies;*

❧ through what other characters say about them;

❧ through what they do, their actions.

As you read the play, examine the following scenes for what they reveal about Gertrude's character and fill in the chart briefly using your own words. If you need more room, use the back of the page.

Scene	What Gertrude says, does, or what others say about her	What this reveals about Gertrude's character
Act V, scene i Ophelia's funeral		
Act V, scene ii Hamlet scores the first hit		

**During-reading Activity
for
Hamlet
Guide to Character Development: Claudius
*Act V***

Shakespeare reveals his characters in four ways:

🔊 through what the characters say to other characters in dialogue;

🔊 through what the characters reveal about their thoughts through long speeches to the audience called *soliloquies;*

🔊 through what other characters say about them;

🔊 through what they do, their actions.

As you read the play, examine the following scenes for what they reveal about Claudius' character and fill in the chart briefly using your own words. If you need more room, use the back of the page.

Scene	What Claudius says, does, or what others say about him	What this reveals about Claudius' character
Act V, scene i Ophelia's funeral		
Act V, scene ii Hamlet scores the first hit		
Act V, scene ii Laertes reveals the conspiracy		

©1994 by The Center for Applied Research in Education

During-reading Activity
for
Hamlet
Guide to Character Development: Horatio
Act V

Shakespeare reveals his characters in four ways:

→ through what the characters say to other characters in dialogue;

→ through what the characters reveal about their thoughts through long speeches to the audience called *soliloquies*;

→ through what other characters say about them;

→ through what they do, their actions.

As you read the play, examine the following scenes for what they reveal about Horatio's character and fill in the chart briefly using your own words. If you need more room, use the back of the page.

Scene	*What Horatio says, does, or what others say about him*	*What this reveals about Horatio's character*
Act V, scene i Hamlet and Horatio encounter the gravedigger and the sexton		
Act V, scene ii Hamlet recounts his adventure at sea and shares his thoughts about Claudius		
Act V, scene ii Hamlet dies		

199

During-reading Activity
for
Hamlet
Guide to Character Development: Laertes
Act V

Shakespeare reveals his characters in four ways:

≈ through what the characters say to other characters in dialogue;

≈ through what the characters reveal about their thoughts through long speeches to the audience called *soliloquies*;

≈ through what other characters say about them;

≈ through what they do, their actions.

As you read the play, examine the following scenes for what they reveal about Laertes' character and fill in the chart briefly using your own words. If you need more room, use the back of the page.

Scene	What Laertes says, does, or what others say about him	What this reveals about Laertes' character
Act V, scene ii Hamlet scores the first hit		
Act V, scene ii Hamlet wounds Laertes		

©1994 by The Center for Applied Research in Education

NAME:_____   DATE:_____

Postreading Activity
for
Hamlet
Comprehension Check
Act V

Directions: After you've read all of Act V, use the following questions to check how well you've understood what you've read. For each question, select the most appropriate answer from the choices listed below it. Place the letter corresponding to your answer in the space to the left of the item number.

____1.   According to the gravedigger, Ophelia is getting a Christian burial because

A. she committed suicide.
B. she is a gentlewoman.
C. she was engaged to Hamlet.
D. Claudius ordered it.
E. she was murdered.

____2.   What does Claudius do to ensure that Laertes will win the fencing match?

A. He orders Laertes to put poison on his dagger and sword.
B. He pays Osric to stab Hamlet from behind.
C. He poisons Hamlet's wine.
D. He bribes the judge.
E. He plans to exile Hamlet if he wins.

____3.   Why does Hamlet jump into Ophelia's open grave?

A. To prove that he is insane.
B. To rescue Laertes.
C. To shame Claudius and Gertrude.
D. To demonstrate that he loved Ophelia as much as Laertes.
E. As punishment for murdering Polonius.

___4.　What does Hamlet conclude about Claudius in the following lines?

ૐ

> *Does it not, think thee, stand me now upon—*
> *He that hath killed my King, and whored my mother;*
> *Popped in between th' election and my hopes,*
> *Thrown out his angle for my proper life,*
> *And with such cozenage—is't not perfect conscience*
> *To quit him with this arm?*

ૐ

A. That Hamlet is justified in killing Claudius.
B. That Hamlet has enough evidence to convict Claudius of the murder of his father.
C. That Hamlet should rejoice in thwarting Claudius' plot to kill him.
D. That Claudius murdered King Hamlet.
E. That Claudius raped Gertrude.

___5.　Why does Claudius' betting on the outcome of the fencing match entice Hamlet to accept the challenge?

A. By taking the heavy odds against Hamlet, Claudius suggests that Hamlet should lose the match.
B. Claudius bets that Laertes will win.
C. By taking the heavy odds against Laertes, Claudius will win more if Hamlet loses.
D. Claudius promises to commit suicide if Hamlet wins.
E. Claudius promises to step down as king if Hamlet wins.

NAME:_____   DATE:_____

Postreading Activity
for
Hamlet
Small Group Discussion Questions to Check Comprehension
Act V

Directions: After you've read all of Act V, discuss each of the following questions briefly in small groups. Use the space below each question to note points you may want to share later. If you need more room, use the back of the page.

1. What complaint do the gravedigger and sexton have as they prepare Ophelia's grave?

2. Why does Hamlet feel that the gravedigger is "a complete knave"?

3. Why does Hamlet jump into Ophelia's grave?

4. What did Hamlet learn about Claudius as a result of his interrupted voyage to England?

5. What prompts Laertes to reveal Claudius' plan to poison Hamlet?

Postreading Activity
for
Hamlet
Critical Thinking Questions
Act V

Directions: To help you develop your understanding of Act V, as your teacher directs you, take time to think about and discuss these questions. The first question is the focus question and is the point of the discussion. Don't be concerned that you may not be able to answer this question at first. Proceed to the exploration questions and then return to the focus question.

Focus Question. As compared to other works of literature, what makes or prevents the resolution of *Hamlet* from being either satisfying or unsatisfying to you as a reader?

Exploration Questions.

1. Under what circumstances were your carefully made plans foiled by unforeseen factors?

2. Although the ending of the play takes several ironic twists, how do the multiple deaths resolve many of the play's conflicts?

3. In what other works of literature does an ironic ending resolve the conflict?

4. In what ways did (or didn't) the final resolution of the play surprise you?

5. Which other works of literature have had especially satisfying (or unsatisfying) resolutions for you as a reader?

6. How does the resolution of *Hamlet* compare with the resolution of conflict in other works of literature that you're familiar with?

©1994 by The Center for Applied Research in Education

Postreading Activity
for
Hamlet
Language Exploration
Irony
Act V

Imagine that while you're in the school cafeteria, someone drops his tray. One of your friends begins applauding and yells out "Way to go, Grace!" More than likely, you'll probably begin to laugh because there's a discrepancy between what your friend said and what she meant. Dropping the tray is not a sign of graceful coordination. When we say one thing and mean another, it is an example of *verbal irony*. Verbal irony is often used in literature. Either the author or a character may say one thing and mean another. This is often the case in Shakespeare's plays.

For example, in Hamlet, Act V, scene ii, Hamlet mentions seeing his dead father to Horatio although Hamlet is unaware that Horatio has come to tell him about the ghost:

My father—methinks I see my father
... In my mind's eye, Horatio.

Shakespeare also use *situational irony*. Situational irony occurs when a discrepancy exists between what a character says and what the character does, or a discrepancy between what a character expects to happen and what does happen.

For example, in Act I, scene iii, Polonius urges Laertes to set sail for France immediately, for the winds are right. However, Polonius also delays Laertes further by giving him extensive advice about how to live away from home.

Directions: The following passages contain examples of verbal and situational irony. Working in pairs, small groups, or as your teacher directs, review each passage in the context of the play and determine the difference between what is said or done and what is expected.

1. Polonius advising Ophelia to be cautious in giving her tenders to Hamlet (Act I, scene iii):

Marry I will teach you; think yourself a baby,
That you have ta'en these tenders for true pay
Which are not sterling. Tender yourself more dearly.

> *Or—not to crack the wind of the poor phrase*
> *Tend'ring it thus you'll tender me a fool.*

≈

2.   Hamlet to Horatio while waiting for the ghost to appear (Act I, scene iv):

≈

> *The King doth wake to-night and takes his rouse*

≈

3.   The ghost telling Hamlet about his death (Act I, scene v):

≈

> *'Tis given out that sleeping in my orchard*
> *A serpent stung me, so the whole ear of Denmark*
> *Is by a forged process of my death*
> *Rankly abused; but know, thou noble youth,*
> *The serpent that did sting thy father's life*
> *Now wears the crown.*

≈

4.   Polonius to Reynaldo (Act II, scene i):

≈

> *But breathe his faults so quaintly,*
> *That they may seem the taints of liberty*

≈

5.   Ophelia describing a strange visit from Hamlet (Act II, scene i):

ↄ

He took me by the wrist, and held me hard;
Then goes he to the length of all his arm,
And with his other hand thus o'er his brow,
He falls to such perusal of my face
As 'a would draw it. Long stayed he so;
At last, a little shaking of mine arm,
And thrice his head thus waving up and down,
He raised a sigh so piteous and profound
As it did seem to shatter all his bulk,
And end his being; that done, he lets me go . . .

ↄ

6.   Claudius to Rosencrantz and Guildenstern (Act II, scene ii):

ↄ

What it should be,
More than his father's death, that thus hath put him
So much from th' understanding of himself,
I cannot dream of. I entreat you both,
That being of so young days brought up with him,
. . .
To draw him on to pleasures, and to gather
So much as from occasion you may glean,
Whether aught to us unknown affects him thus . . .

ↄ

7. Claudius rising from his attempts at prayer (Act III, scene iii):

&

My words fly up, my thoughts remain below.
Words without thoughts never to heaven go.

&

8. Gertrude confronting Hamlet (Act III, scene iv):

&

Hamlet, thou hast thy father much offended.

&

9. Hamlet replying to Rosencrantz and Guildenstern's request to know the location of Polonius' body (Act IV, scene ii):

&

The body is with the King, but the King is not with the body.

&

10. Gertrude drinking to Hamlet's scoring first (Act V, scene ii):

&

The Queen arouses to thy fortune, Hamlet.

&

©1994 by The Center for Applied Research in Education

Language Exploration Review
Hamlet

Directions: Now that you've discussed all the Language Exploration Activities, use the following questions to check how well you can apply what you've learned to new selections. For each question, select the most appropriate answer from the choices listed below it. Place the letter corresponding to your answer in the space to the left of the item number.

Questions 1 and 2 refer to the following passage:

❧

Haply the seas, and the countries different,
With variable objects, shall expel
This something-settled matter in his heart.

❧

____1.   Which of the following literary devices is Claudius using?

A. metaphor
B. personification
C. apostrophe
D. simile
E. irony

____2.   In the passage, Claudius suggests:

A. Travel will make Hamlet worse.
B. Travel won't make Hamlet any worse.
C. Travel will distract Hamlet, changing his mood.
D. Travel will distract Hamlet but not affect his mood.
E. Travel will distract Hamlet.

Questions 3 and 4 refer to the following passage:

❧

Why now you speak
Like a good child, and a true gentleman.

❧

____3. Which of the following literary devices is Claudius using?

A. metaphor
B. personification
C. apostrophe
D. simile
E. irony

____4. Which idea does Claudius imply about Laertes' behavior:

A. He's stubborn.
B. He's ignorant.
C. He's innocent.
D. He's obedient.
E. He's angry.

Questions 5 and 6 refer to the following passage:

ᴈ

The cess of majesty
Dies not alone; but like a gulf doth draw
What's near it with it. It is a massy wheel
Fixed on the summit of the highest mount,
To whose huge spokes ten thousand lesser things
Are mortised and adjoined.

ᴈ

____5. Which of the following literary devices is Rosencrantz using?

A. metaphor
B. personification
C. apostrophe
D. simile
E. symbol

____6. In this passage, Rosencrantz suggests:

A. Many people may fall if Claudius is deposed.
B. The wheel is overgrown with weeds.
C. The wheel of kingship is slipping.
D. The wheel is approaching the summit.
E. The wheel is broken.

©1994 by The Center for Applied Research in Education

Questions 7 and 8 refer to the following passage:

❧

But howsoever thou pursues this act,
Taint not thy mind, nor let they soul contrive
Against they mother aught; leave her to heaven,
And to those thorns that in her bosom lodge
To prick and sting her.

❧

___7.   Which sense does the passage appeal to?

A. sight
B. smell
C. taste
D. touch
E. hearing

___8.   In the passage, what does the ghost suggest to Hamlet?

A. To take vengeance upon Gertrude, too.
B. To leave the judgment of Gertrude to God.
C. To beg Gertrude to confess her sins.
D. That Gertrude is as guilty as Claudius.
E. Hamlet should forgive Gertrude's actions.

Questions 9 and 10 refer to the following passage:

❧

When in your motion you are hot and dry,
And make your bouts more violent to that end,
And that he calls for drink, I'll have prepared him
A chalice for the nonce, whereon sipping,
If he by chance escape your venomed stuck,
Our purpose may hold there.

❧

___9.   Which of the following literary devices is Claudius using?

A. irony
B. personification
C. apostrophe
D. simile
E. symbol

211

____10. Which situation does Claudius unknowingly set up in this passage?

    A. The only means for his own death.
    B. The only means for Gertrude's death.
    C. The means for Laertes' and Gertrude's deaths.
    D. The means for Hamlet's death.
    E. The means for his own and Gertrude's deaths.

Postreading Activity
for
Hamlet
Vocabulary in Context
Act V

Directions: In each of the passages below you will find one of the words from the prereading vocabulary list for Act V. Review the definitions given in the prereading vocabulary. Working individually, in pairs, or in small groups as your teacher directs, examine each of the underlined words in the following passages from Act V. For each word, use the appropriate meaning and develop a brief interpretation of the passage within the context of the play.

____1.   Hamlet commenting on the gravedigger's character (scene i):

æ

How <u>absolute</u> the knave is! We must speak by the card, or equivocation will undo us.

æ

____2.   Hamlet pondering Yorick's skull (scene i):

æ

Alas poor Yorick! I knew him Horatio, a fellow of infinite jest, of most excellent <u>fancy</u>.

æ

213

___3.   Hamlet reacting to Ophelia's funeral procession (scene i):

ক্ষ

Who is this they follow?
And with such <u>maimed</u> rites? This doth betoken
The corse they follow did with desperate hand
Fordo it own life.

ক্ষ

___4.   Laertes leaping into Ophelia's open grave (scene i):

ক্ষ

Now pile your dust upon the <u>quick</u> and dead,
Till of this flat a mountain you have made
T' o'ertop old Pelion or the skyish head
Of blue Olympus.

ক্ষ

___5.   Hamlet challenging Laertes at Ophelia's funeral (scene i):

ক্ষ

Dost come here to whine,
To <u>outface</u> me with leaping in her grave?
Be buried quick with her, and so will I.

ক্ষ

©1994 by The Center for Applied Research in Education

___6.   Hamlet to Horatio, commenting upon his discovery of Claudius' plot
to have Rosencrantz and Guildenstern kill Hamlet (scene ii):

ࡔ

> *Rashly—*
> *And praised be rashness for it; let us know,*
> *Our <u>indiscretion</u> sometime serves us well*
> *When our deep plots do pall, and that should learn us*
> *There's a divinity that shapes our ends,*
> *Rough-hew them how we will.*

ࡔ

___7.   Hamlet to Horatio (scene ii):

ࡔ

> *Up from my cabin,*
> *My sea-gown <u>scarfed</u> about me,*

ࡔ

___8.   Hamlet to Horatio (scene ii):

ࡔ

> *. . . in the dark*
> *Groped I to find out them, had my desire,*
> *Fingered their <u>packet</u>, and in fine withdrew*
> *To mine own room again;*

ࡔ

____9. Hamlet to Horatio about Claudius' plot (scene ii):

৵

He that hath killed my King, and whored my mother;
Popped in between th' election and my hopes,
Thrown out his <u>angle</u> for my proper life,
And with such cozenage—is't not perfect conscience
To quit him with this arm?

৵

____10. Osric to Hamlet (scene ii):

৵

The King sir, hath wagered with him six Barbary horses, against the
which he has imponed, as I take it, six French rapiers and poniards,
with their assigns, as girdle, hangers, and so. Three of the <u>carriages</u> in
faith are very dear to fancy, very responsive to the hilts, most delicate
<u>carriages</u> and very liberal conceit.

৵

Vocabulary Review Quiz
for
Hamlet
Act V

Directions: For each of the italicized words in the sentences below, determine which letter best reflects the use of the word in this context. Place the letter corresponding to your answer in the space to the left of the item number.

_____1. When Hamlet refers to the gravedigger as an *absolute* knave, he means

A. completely disrespectful   B. completely loyal   C. completely insane   D. completely unworthy   E. completely brave

_____2. When Hamlet praised Yorick's *fancy*, he was referring to his

A. clothing   B. wealth   C. home   D. imagination   E. concern for children

_____3. To *maim* means to

A. defeat   B. render powerless   C. beat senseless   D. organize skillfully   E. rank in order of importance

_____4. When Laertes refers to the *quick* at Ophelia's funeral, he means

A. the swift   B. the emotional   C. the living   D. the dead   E. the famous

_____5. When Hamlet accuses Laertes of trying to *outface* him, he means that Laertes was trying to

A. outrun him   B. shame him   C. overshadow him   D. overcome him   E. usurp his throne

_____6. For Hamlet, *indiscretion* means

A. ungrateful actions   B. unguarded behaviors   C. unlawful conduct   D. uninvolved attitudes   E. unproductive actions

_____7. To *scarf* means to

A. eat quickly   B. subdue   C. wrap   D. secure with rope   E. demand

_____8. When Hamlet refers to *packet*, he means

A. a small package   B. a plot   C. a boat   D. a disease   E. a battle

____9. When Hamlet refers to Claudius' *angle*, he means

A. a particular viewpoint   B. a special dispensation   C. a baited hook   D. a straightforward manner   E. an unwillingness to change

____10. Part of Claudius' bet includes *carriages* which are

A. ornate carts   B. scabbards   C. ornamental sword hilts   D. decorative supports for scabbards   E. blades etched elaborately

EXTENDING ACTIVITIES

NAME:_____   DATE:_____

Overview of
Extending Activities
for *Hamlet*

Directions: Now that you've completed your formal study of *Hamlet*, the extending activities listed below will provide you with opportunities to extend your understanding of the play. Remember that these are suggestions of things you might do. Perhaps you will think of others or your teacher may have additional suggestions. Your teacher can provide you with specific sets of directions for *acting out, oral interpretation, puppet theater, masks, writing assignments,* and *visual displays.*

Acting Out

1. Dramatize a missing scene related to the characters and situations in the play. For example, the visit that Hamlet makes to Ophelia that she describes to Polonius in Act II, scene i.

2. Present a scene from the play in a modern context. Use contemporary settings, words, and ideas. For example, what might Hamlet's "To be or not to be" soliloquy sound like as a rap lyric?

Oral Inter-pretation

Present a prepared reading of the speech of a single character, between two characters, or of an entire scene. Keep in mind that oral interpretation involves communicating words effectively *without* actually memorizing a script and acting out a scene with full costumes and props.

Puppet Theater

Make paper bag puppets and use them to present a scene from the play.

Masks

Create paper plate masks for specific characters and present a scene from the play using them.

Writing Assignments

1. Write an alternative ending to the play.

2. Research some element of Danish life in the time of Hamlet (c. 1200 A.D.) or the time of Shakespeare (approximately 1600 A.D.).

3. Using the character diary you kept while reading the play, write a letter or note from your character to another character in the play or to a relative in a neighboring country.

Visual Displays

1. Create a graffiti wall for Elsinore that reflects a specific time during the play.

2. Create a time line for the play where you list the significant events in order.

3. Draw a comic strip or drawing for a scene from the play.

4. Create a filmstrip or video related to the play.

5. Construct a mobile using double-sided objects/characters from the play with a 3 × 5 card containing a description beneath each object.

6. Create a music video combining still pictures with music and words.

7. Select and depict 12 to 16 scenes from the play for a multiple panel quilt. Make each panel out of paper. For each panel of your quilt, create an illustration and write a caption that explains it. Create a border for each panel and tie or string them together using clothesline or heavy string to form a large wall hanging.

8. Research and build a Globe Theater model.

9. Research and present samples of Danish cooking.

10. Research and present how Elizabethan actors may have interpreted Danish costumes.

11. Create a slide sound presentation on some aspect of the play.

NAME:_____   DATE:_____

Extending Activities
for
Hamlet
Acting Out

Directions: From time to time during your study of *Hamlet,* you may have participated in an improvised scene from the play either before or after you read particular scenes. Now that you've read the entire play, here are some additional opportunities for you to act out and demonstrate your fuller understanding of the play and its characters. You may want to improvise these scenes or to fully script and rehearse them.

1. Suppose you were Francisco, Barnardo, or Marcellus. How would you tell Horatio about seeing the ghost on the battlements?

2. Suppose you were the psychologist to whom Hamlet has come during Act I of the play. How would you help him sort out his feelings of ambiguity toward Gertrude and Claudius?

3. The afternoon following Act I, scene v, Hamlet visits Ophelia, pretending to be insane.

4. Sometime between Act III, scene iv (where Hamlet kills Polonius) and Act IV, scene v (Ophelia's mad scene), someone informs Laertes about his father's death. Improvise the scene where the messenger brings Laertes the news.

5. In an additional scene after the end of the play, Fortinbras appears before the people to let them know that he is the new King of Denmark and that when he becomes King of Norway he will join the kingdoms together. What does he say?

6. Create a scene in Heaven or Hell where specific characters defend their lives or tell others what has happened in their lives. You may want to include King Hamlet along with the other characters in the play.

7. Reynaldo meets "other Danskers" when he arrives in Paris. What tales does he invent about Laertes to win their confidence? (You may want to refer to Polonius' instructions to Laertes [Act I, scene iii] and to his instructions to Reynaldo [Act II, scene ii].)

8. Gertrude informs Ophelia of the death of her father. What does she say?

9. Develop a segment for "60 Minutes," CBS, NBC, or ABC Evening News, "Entertainment Tonight," "Phil Donahue," "Oprah," "Geraldo," "Now It Can Be Told," or "A Current Affair" based upon *Hamlet*.

10. The gravedigger and the sexton, who appear in Act V, scene i, are in one of their kitchens the day that Claudius and Gertrude marry. What are their views on the events of the day?

Extending Activities
for
Hamlet
Oral Interpretation

Directions: Present a prepared reading of a speech or scene from *Hamlet*. Listed below are suggestions of scenes for one, two, or three or more actors to choose from. You may want to check with your teacher and present other scenes. To help you prepare your scene, work through all the steps.

One-Actor Scenes

Hamlet, Act I, sc. ii—"O that this too too solid flesh would melt . . ."

Claudius, Act I, sc. ii—opening speech relating the exposition

Hamlet, Act III, sc. ii—Hamlet's advice to actors (omit player's lines)

Claudius, Act III, sc. ii—Claudius' confession

Hamlet, Act IV, sc. iv—Hamlet's soliloquy

Two-Actor Scenes

Laertes and Ophelia, Act I, sc. iii—Laertes' advice to Ophelia

Hamlet and ghost, Act I, sc. v—the ghost tells his story

Polonius and Reynaldo, Act II, sc. i—Polonius gives Reynaldo instructions about Laertes' education

Polonius and Ophelia, Act II, sc. i—Ophelia tells her father about Hamlet's visit

Hamlet and Polonius, Act II, sc. ii—Hamlet calls Polonius a fishmonger

Hamlet and Ophelia, Act III, sc. i—Hamlet and Ophelia's meeting

Hamlet and Gertrude, Act III, sc. iii—Hamlet confronts Gertrude (following the murder of Polonius)

Claudius and Gertrude, Act IV, sc. i—Gertrude tells Claudius of Polonius' death

Claudius and Laertes, Act IV, sc. vii—the plot to kill Hamlet

Gravedigger and sexton, Act V, sc. i—up to Hamlet's entrance

Hamlet and sexton, Act V, sc. i—through the end of Hamlet's "Alas poor Yorick!" speech

Hamlet and Horatio, Act V, sc. ii—up to Osric's entrance

Scenes for Three or
More Actors

> Hamlet, Horatio, Marcellus, Act I, sc. ii—Horatio and Marcellus tell Hamlet about the ghost
>
> Claudius, Gertrude, Rosencrantz, Guildenstern, Act II, scene ii—The King and Queen enlist the aid of Rosencrantz and Guildenstern
>
> Claudius, Gertrude, Polonius, Act II, sc. ii—Polonius explains what's causing Hamlet's problems
>
> Hamlet, Rosencrantz, Guildenstern, Act II, sc. ii—Hamlet sees through Rosencrantz and Guildenstern's plan to spy for Claudius
>
> Claudius, Rosencrantz, Guildenstern, Gertrude, Act III, sc. i—Rosencrantz and Guildenstern admit that they learned nothing from Hamlet
>
> Ophelia, Claudius, Laertes, Act IV, sc. v—Ophelia's mad scene

Steps for
Preparing an
Oral Interpretation

1. Select a scene or passage that you really like. The passage should have a definite beginning, high point, and end. Remember that you will be doing a prepared reading and not memorizing a script. Most often, oral interpreters either stand before their audiences or sit on stools.

2. Prepare a script to work from. You may want to type out the selection or Xerox it from a book. You'll need a copy that you can make notes on. Mount your script on black or other dark construction paper, so that you can read from it easily without having to hold it with both hands. Keep the pages of your manuscript loose, so you can either slide them out of the way or shift them under each other as you finish reading them.

3. Analyze the script. As you work through the analysis, make notes to yourself in pencil on your script.

    a. Read the whole passage and decide what it's about. Because you've already read the whole play, you know where your selection fits into the development of the characters.

    b. Read the whole piece several times and decide what the overall effect of the piece is.

    c. Make notes of things you don't understand—allusions, words, and so forth. Check the footnotes in your text or look up unfamiliar words in the dictionary. Remember that the meaning of particular words may have changed since Shakespeare's time. If you have a problem understanding a particular word, check the glossary of terms found in most *Complete Works of Shakespeare* plays in your library.

d. As you look at individual words, you should know how to pronounce all of them as well as know both their denotative meaning (the dictionary meaning) and their connotative meaning (the emotional subtleties that come from using the word in a particular context).

e. Where does the scene take place? Is it a public place, like the great hall of the castle, or a private one like Gertrude's chamber? Who speaks, and what is the speaker's emotional state at the time? What has happened before this scene?

f. Examine the overall organization of the scene. What emotions do the characters reveal? What changes in character, motivation, or emotions occur? For example, in Claudius' opening speech, his demeanor shifts with his subject matter. Decide how you can convey these changes with your voice.

4. Begin practicing aloud. Read the passage out loud, working either with a partner or with a tape recorder. Listen to yourself. Experiment with different readings. Underline words you would like to emphasize. Make marginal notes about the emotions you would like to portray in different parts.

5. Write a brief introduction to your scene, setting it up for your listeners. The following example could be used to introduce Act V, scene i:

∂

As the gravedigger and the sexton prepare Ophelia's grave, they comment on the privileges of being an aristocrat.

∂

6. Once you've decided on how you would like to read your selection, practice, practice, practice! Your goal in these sessions is not to memorize words, but to learn interpretation, so that when you do your presentation, you can concentrate on a smooth performance.

7. Perform the piece. Some interpreters prefer to stand while others prefer to sit upon stools. You may hold the script in your hands or use a music stand or lectern.

Extending Activities
for
Hamlet
Puppet Theater

©1994 by The Center for Applied Research in Education

One way to present scenes from *Hamlet* without having to worry about elaborate sets or costumes is to use puppets made from brown paper bags. You can make your own puppets using construction paper, scissors, rubber cement, crayons, and felt-tip markers. You can use a table turned sideways as a stage for the puppeteers to hide behind. If you feel that you need scenery, make a mural and use masking tape to secure it to the wall behind you.

*Steps to Making
and Performing Scenes
with Puppets:*

1. Select a scene that you want to perform. Listed below are scenes for two, and three or more actors.

*Two-Actor
Scenes*

Laertes and Ophelia, Act I, sc. iii—Laertes' advice to Ophelia

Hamlet and ghost, Act I, sc. v—the ghost tells his story

Polonius and Reynaldo, Act II, sc. i—Polonius gives Reynaldo instructions about Laertes' education

Polonius and Ophelia, Act II, sc. i—Ophelia tells her father about Hamlet's visit

Hamlet and Polonius, Act II, sc. ii—Hamlet calls Polonius a fishmonger

Hamlet and Ophelia, Act III, sc. i—Hamlet and Ophelia's meeting

Hamlet and Gertrude, Act III, sc. iii—Hamlet confronts Gertrude (following the murder of Polonius)

Claudius and Gertrude, Act IV, sc. i—Gertrude tells Claudius of Polonius' death

Claudius and Laertes, Act IV, sc. vii—the plot to kill Hamlet

Gravedigger and sexton, Act V, sc. i—up to Hamlet's entrance

Hamlet and sexton, Act V, sc. i—through the end of Hamlet's "Alas poor Yorick" speech

Hamlet and Horatio, Act V, sc. ii—up to Osric's entrance

*Scenes for
Three or
More Actors*

Hamlet, Horatio, Marcellus, Act I, sc. ii—Horatio and Marcellus tell Hamlet about the ghost

228

Claudius, Gertrude, Rosencrantz, Guildenstern, Act II, sc. ii—The King and Queen enlist the aid of Rosencrantz and Guildenstern

Claudius, Gertrude, Polonius, Act II, sc. ii—Polonius explains what's causing Hamlet's problems

Hamlet, Rosencrantz, Guildenstern, Act II, sc. ii—Hamlet sees through Rosencrantz and Guildenstern's plan to spy for Claudius

Claudius, Rosencrantz, Guildenstern, Gertrude, Act III, sc. i—Rosencrantz and Guildenstern admit they learned nothing from Hamlet

Ophelia, Claudius, Laertes, Act IV, sc. v—Ophelia's mad scene

2. Design and make puppets. In making your puppets, refer to *Figure 1*. To make your puppet talk, insert your hand into the bag and curl your fingers so the upper face on the top of the bag moves up and down.

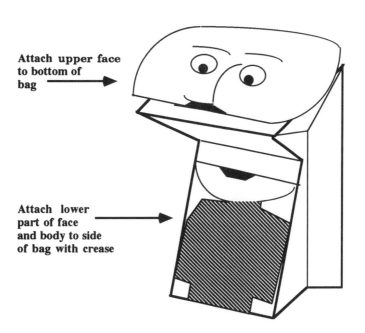

Attach upper face to bottom of bag →

Attach lower part of face and body to side of bag with crease →

Figure 1
Paper Bag Puppet

3. Prepare your script as if you were doing an oral interpretation. See specific directions entitled Extending Activity for *Hamlet*: Oral Interpretation.

4. Decide how you can make your puppet appear to walk and move.

5. Practice, practice, practice.

Extending Activities
for
Hamlet
Paper Plate Masks

Directions: One way to help you present scenes from Hamlet is to create a half-mask to represent a character from a specific scene. When you present your scene, hold the mask in front of you to create the character.

To make your own mask, you will need

large white paper plates (do not use plastic plates)
large craft stick
scissors
glue (either rubber cement or hot melt glue gun work well)
assorted construction paper, ribbon, cloth, cardboard, yarn to make hair, hats
 and other decorations that help represent the character
crayons, colored pencils, or felt-tip markers

Assemble the mask as illustrated in *Figure 2*.

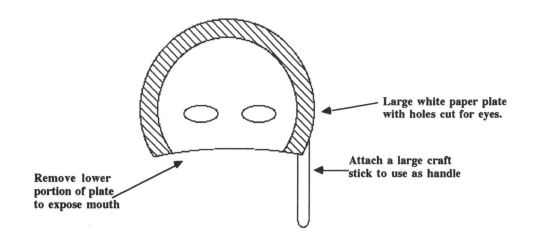

Large white paper plate
with holes cut for eyes.

Attach a large craft
stick to use as handle

Remove lower
portion of plate
to expose mouth

Figure 2
Paper Plate Mask

Extending Activities
for
Hamlet
Writing Assignments

Directions: Given below are some ideas for possible writing assignments based on your understanding of the characters and situations in *Hamlet*.

1. You are the casting director for a new rock version of *Hamlet*. Write a letter to the film's producers explaining who from among current film, television, and rock and roll stars you would like to cast in each of the play's principal roles: Hamlet, Ophelia, Laertes, Polonius, Claudius, and Gertrude.

2. Write Ophelia's letter of farewell to Hamlet.

3. Write a new or more satisfying ending to the play.

4. Create a "Meeting of Minds" where characters from *Hamlet* interact with characters from other works of literature. You may also want to have the characters interact with their authors.

5. Create a children's version of the play. Check *Shake Hands with Shakespeare* or Charles and Caroline Lamb's *Tales from Shakespeare*.

6. Create an illustrated children's book based upon *Hamlet*.

7. Write Fortinbras' eulogy for Hamlet.

8. Investigate the Globe Theater restoration project in London and report your findings to the class.

9. Research the food, clothing, housing, festivals or celebrations for either Elizabethan England or Denmark during the time of *Hamlet* (approximately 1200 A.D.).

10. Using the character diary that you kept during your reading of the play, write a letter to your cousin in Paris relaying both the events of the play and your response to them.

11. As one of the characters in the play, write a letter to either "Dear Abby" or "Ann Landers," and imagine the columnist's reply.

12. Research the development and historical aspect of weapons used at either the time of *Hamlet* (1200 A.D.) or in Shakespeare's time (1600 A.D.).

PART THREE

Appendices

Appendix A

EVALUATING READING PROCESS ACTIVITIES

This section will show you how to evaluate and assign grades for reading process activities for a unit on *Hamlet,* and how to set up and review reading activity folders. It also reviews the instructional goals for all activities and suggests specific guidelines for evaluating them.

ASSESSING STUDENTS' PARTICIPATION

With a reading workshop approach to literature, just as with a writing workshop approach to written composition, you must decide how to assess the students' participation in process activities and to evaluate the formal products that demonstrate learning as well. The activities in this resource provide opportunities for students to improve their reading, writing, speaking, listening, and critical thinking processes while they study *Hamlet.* Although you don't need to grade all the process activities formally, you will want to review and respond to your students' work as they read the play. If you and your students were to devote approximately three weeks to a unit on *Hamlet,* you might use the percentages listed in the table below.

SUGGESTED COMPONENTS OF UNIT GRADE

Activity	Percentage of Unit Grade	Numbers of Items and Point Values	Total
		(Intro with videotape and 9	
Prereading activities	10%	reading sessions @ 5 pts.)	50 pts.
Response journals or character diaries	20%	(5 [one per act] @ 20 pts.)	100 pts.
Postreading activities	10%	(5 summary sessions @ 10 pts.)	50 pts.
Comprehension checks	10%	(5 @ 10 pts.)	50 pts.
Vocabulary review quizzes	10%	(5 @ 10 pts.)	50 pts.
Language exploration activities	10%	(5 @ 10 pts.)	50 pts.
Language exploration review quiz	5%		25 pts.
Individual or group extending activity	25%		125 pts.
Total	100%		**500 pts.**

SETTING UP AND REVIEWING READING ACTIVITY FOLDERS

Reading folders allow the students to keep their prereading, during-reading, and postreading activities together for the entire unit. Any type of folder works well although two pocket folders allow for storage of response journals or character diaries on one side and other reading process activities on the other.

To monitor the students' progress and to provide formative evaluation, review approximately 20 percent of the students' folders for each class period at the end of each day. Select the folders at random, so the class doesn't know when you will check any individual's work. Take a few minutes to skim and scan the work in each folder.

As you review each student's work, check to see that the student understands the directions and purpose of each activity. Use brief comments to praise the work specifically and to point out specific deficiencies. Then record the date of your review and any point values. You might try using +✓ for outstanding work, ✓ for satisfactory work, and –✓ for less than satisfactory work because students may find these symbols less threatening than traditional letter grades. You can translate codes like these into a numerical equivalent for your records: for example, awarding 5 points for outstanding work, 4 for satisfactory, and 3 for less than satisfactory.

INSTRUCTIONAL GOALS AND EVALUATIVE GUIDELINES FOR SPECIFIC READING ACTIVITIES

This section states both the instructional goals for specific reading process activities and suggests ways to assess them.

Focusing Activities

Although students complete only *one* focusing activity for a particular scene, all focusing activities share two common *instructional goals:*

ᴥ to organize student's prior knowledge related to *Hamlet;*

ᴥ to establish a purpose for reading a scene.

Scenarios for Improvisation

Guidelines for Assessment:

Does the student

ᴥ participate as either actor or audience actively?

ᴥ provide logical motivations for character's actions?

ᴥ establish actions that are consistent with setting and existing information about character?

Prereading Discussion Questions

Guidelines for Assessment:

Does the student

- ❧ participate in discussion?

- ❧ share ideas willingly?

- ❧ allow others to share ideas?

- ❧ provide explanation or support for ideas?

- ❧ provide speculations that are consistent with the student's existing knowledge of *Hamlet*?

Speculation Journal

Guidelines for Assessment:

Does the student

- ❧ address the issues contained in the question(s)?

- ❧ provide explanation or support for ideas?

- ❧ provide speculations that are consistent with the student's existing knowledge of *Hamlet*?

Introducing the Play with Videotape

Guidelines for Assessment:

Does the student

- ❧ attempt to answer all the questions?

- ❧ address the issues in the questions?

- ❧ have an overall understanding of the scene and its conflict?

Vocabulary

Instructional Goals:

- ❧ to review definitions of less familiar words

- ❧ to demonstrate the effect of context upon meaning

Plot Summaries

Instructional Goals:

- ъ to establish an overview of each scene

- ъ to provide a reference for the student when Shakespeare's text seems incomprehensible

Response Journals

As one of two ongoing writing-to-learn activities that students may use during their reading of *Hamlet*, the response journal has two *instructional goals:*

- ъ to summarize and reflect upon the meaning of the play;

- ъ to recognize, record, and comment upon repeated elements found in the play, such as symbols, motifs, themes, character development, or figurative language.

Guidelines for Assessment:

Does the student

- ъ record an entry for each reading session?

- ъ meet minimum length requirements for each entry?

- ъ respond emotionally, associatively, figuratively?

- ъ demonstrate an accurate understanding of the literary facts of *Hamlet*?

- ъ demonstrate an honest effort to begin making sense of the play and developing an understanding of it?

- ъ probe responses and attempt to understand them rather than only summarize or paraphrase the action of the play?

Character Diary

As one of two ongoing writing-to-learn activities that students may use during their reading of *Hamlet,* the character diary has two *instructional goals:*

- ъ to summarize and reflect upon the meaning of the play;

- ъ to begin to evaluate the action of the play from the perspective of an individual character.

Guidelines for Assessment:

Does the student

- ✍︎ record an entry for each reading session?

- ✍︎ meet minimum length requirements for each entry?

- ✍︎ provide an account for how the character learns of the action of the scene(s) just read?

- ✍︎ demonstrate an accurate understanding of the literary facts of *Hamlet*?

- ✍︎ demonstrate an honest effort to begin making sense of the play and developing an understanding of it?

- ✍︎ probe responses and attempt to understand them rather than only summarize or paraphrase the action of the play?

Viewing a Scene on Videotape

Unlike using a scene to introduce *Hamlet*, viewing a scene after students have read it provides additional information that may help them to understand the text of the play.

Instructional Goals:

- ✍︎ to recognize that the performance of a scene affects the student's understanding, comprehension, and interpretation of it;

- ✍︎ to compare and contrast a student's interpretation of a scene with the performers'.

Guidelines for Assessment:

Does the student

- ✍︎ attempt to answer all the questions?

- ✍︎ address the issues in the questions?

- ✍︎ demonstrate an honest effort to make sense of the presentation?

- ✍︎ begin to make connections between the videotaped presentation and the text of *Hamlet*?

Guides to Character Development

Although students complete these activities after they've read each act, they will re-read and actively contemplate specific portions of the play. The students may examine Hamlet, Claudius, or Gertrude as major characters, and Horatio, Laertes, Ophelia, and Polonius as minor ones.

Instructional Goals:

- ❧ to recognize and identify the means that Shakespeare uses to develop or reveal character;

- ❧ to use evidence from the play to develop and support an interpretation of a character.

Guidelines for Assessment:

Does the student

- ❧ attempt to answer all the questions?

- ❧ address the issues in the questions?

- ❧ use information from the play to develop and support logical conclusions about the characters?

Comprehension Checks

Both the Comprehension Check and the Small Group Discussion Questions provide means to assess the student's reading comprehension.

Comprehension Checks (Multiple Choice)

Instructional Goal:

- ❧ to assess reading comprehension of an entire act through factual, interpretative, and evaluative questions.

Guidelines for Assessment:

- ❧ answer keys appear in Appendix C.

Small Group Discussion Questions

Instructional Goal:

- ❧ to assess reading comprehension of an entire act through factual, interpretative, and evaluative questions.

Guidelines for Assessment:

Does the student

- ❧ participate in discussion?

- attempt to answer all the questions?

- address the issues in the questions?

- use information from the play to develop and support logical conclusions about the play?

Critical Thinking Questions

Instructional Goals:

- to connect the play to the student's life in meaningful ways;

- to evaluate interpretations of the play using textual evidence, personal experience, and knowledge of related literature.

Guidelines for Assessment:

Does the student

- attempt to answer both the exploration questions as well as the focus question?

- appropriately address the issues of each question?

- use specific information to support ideas?

- integrate personal experience, knowledge of related literature, and textual evidence?

- draw logical conclusions from the existing evidence?

Language Exploration Activities

Instructional Goals:

- to review definitions of selected literary devices and examine them within the context of Hamlet.

- to apply knowledge of literary devices with textual evidence to develop and evaluate interpretations of specific passages of *Hamlet*.

Guidelines for Assessment:

Suggested answers appear in Appendix C.

Does the student

- complete the items that the teacher assigns?

- make an effort to apply the definition of the literary device to the lines in the play?

◆ review the passage within the broader context of the individual speech, scene, or play?

◆ provide specific support of interpretation(s)?

Language Exploration Review Quiz

Instructional Goal:

◆ to assess student's understanding of how specific literary devices affect the interpretation of specific passages from *Hamlet*.

Guidelines for Assessment:
Suggested answers appear in Appendix C.
Has the student

◆ completed the preceding language exploration activities?

Vocabulary in Context

Instructional Goals:

◆ to review the additional meanings of words;

◆ to analyze the use of specific words within the context of a particular passage;

◆ to develop interpretations of specific passages, using knowledge and context.

Guidelines for assessment:
Suggested answers appear in Appendix C.
Does the student

◆ complete the items that the teacher assigns?

◆ review the definitions of the words?

◆ make an effort to apply the meaning of the word to the lines in the play?

◆ review the passage within the broader context of the individual speech, scene, or play?

◆ provide specific support for interpretation(s)?

Vocabulary Review Quizzes

Instructional Goal:

◆ to assess the student's understanding of specific words in context.

Guidelines for Assessment:

Suggested answers appear in Appendix C.

Has the student

❧ reviewed the meaning of the words?

❧ completed the preceding vocabulary in context activities?

Individual or Group Extending Activities

Instructional Goals:

❧ to apply a knowledge and understanding of *Hamlet* to new situations and contexts.

❧ to provide additional opportunities for students to apply reading, writing, speaking, listening, viewing, and critical thinking skills.

Guidelines for Assessment:

Does the student

❧ have a purpose and focus for an extending activity that is directly related to the play and the study of it?

❧ present information clearly and logically?

❧ present information, whether from the play or research, accurately and with appropriate documentation?

❧ present interpretations of characters or events from the play that are consistent with the information in the text?

❧ meet all appropriate, additional criteria and specifications that the teacher sets?

Appendix B

USING SMALL GROUPS SUCCESSFULLY

I advocate using small groups throughout this resource. Small groups are a great way to get lots of students involved quickly. Several practices that make these groups operate more effectively:

- Assign students to specific groups. When they self-select their groups, they often socialize rather than focus on the task at hand.

- Mix students of different backgrounds, abilities, and talents. In discussion situations, multiple perspectives often lead to insights.

- Structure the group assignments and provide written directions (on the chalkboard, overhead projector, or in written handouts). When students know their audience and the purpose of the assignment, they tend to stay on task. All members of the group need to understand what their jobs are, what the final product needs to look like, and how much time they have to complete it.

- Establish class rules for small group behavior and encourage students to work together.

- Monitor students' behavior as they work in groups. Move around the room in a random fashion.

Appendix C

ANSWER KEYS

Comprehension Checks

Act I

1. D
2. B
3. E
4. D
5. A

Act II

1. C
2. D
3. B
4. A
5. E

Act III

1. B
2. C
3. D
4. B
5. A

Act IV

1. A
2. C
3. C
4. B
5. C

Act V

1. B
2. C
3. D
4. A
5. A

SUGGESTED ANSWERS FOR SMALL GROUP DISCUSSION QUESTIONS

Act I

1. For Horatio and the soldiers on watch, the ghost may not be the spirit of the dead king; instead, it could be an evil spirit come to lure some mortal to his death or it may be one that wants Hamlet to murder an innocent man, thereby committing a mortal sin and bringing about everlasting damnation.

2. Claudius points out that Hamlet has lost a father, as did his father before him. While it's necessary for kings to grieve for their own fathers, these same deaths are also the means by which new kings succeed the throne.

3. Laertes warns his sister not to be too willing to believe what Hamlet might say or write. He may say that he loves her, but he is after all in line to be king, so his choices for marriage are not necessarily his own. Besides, he may just be trying to win her trust to have sex.

4. Ophelia is an obedient daughter of the Elizabethan age and agrees not to see Hamlet or receive his letters.

5. Hamlet suggests that he may have to act strangely to test the truth of the ghost's story. He swears all to secrecy, so no one else will know the ghost's version of the death of King Hamlet.

Act II

1. Ophelia has had an encounter with Hamlet, who came to her with his clothing in disarray. He held her face and studied it, sighed deeply, and then left without saying anything. Such strange behavior frightens her.

2. Polonius believes that Hamlet's strange behavior arises from his being mad for love of Ophelia.

3. Claudius hopes that Rosencrantz and Guildenstern, as two of Hamlet's school friends, can gain Hamlet's trust and help determine the cause of Hamlet's strange behavior.

4. Hamlet figures out that Claudius has sent for Rosencrantz and Guildenstern and is determined not to reveal his plan to them. Instead he uses his encounter with them to convince them that he is indeed mad.

5. Hamlet has seen the players perform before and is familiar with their repertoire. He asks the troupe to include a speech that he will write for their performance the following night.

Act III

1. Polonius believes that Hamlet is mad for love of Ophelia. He explains the relationship to the king and queen and even cites quotations from Hamlet's love letters and poetry to Ophelia to support his case. Polonius' plan is to have Ophelia encounter Hamlet "accidentally," while he and Claudius eavesdrop. This way, they can observe Hamlet's behavior directly.

2. Polonius and Claudius reach different conclusions. Claudius believes that Hamlet is afflicted with a deep melancholy that might make him dangerous, so he plans to send Hamlet to England. Polonius still believes that the source of Hamlet's behavior is his love for Ophelia.

3. Hamlet has had the players reenact the murder of his father. When Claudius sees this, he rises and cancels the performance. Hamlet takes this as a sign of Claudius' guilt.

4. After Claudius reveals that he did indeed murder his brother, he kneels to pray for forgiveness. Hamlet fears that if he kills Claudius while he's praying, Claudius will become a martyr and enter Heaven rather than spend eternity in Hell. Ironically, Claudius reveals that his prayers do not work, so Hamlet misses his chance.

5. Hamlet, referring to figures in tapestry, reveals the truth to Gertrude that Claudius murdered King Hamlet. He makes her promise that she will not let Claudius seduce her again, or reveal that he pretends to be mad.

Act IV

1. Claudius is afraid that although Hamlet is viewed as mad, he is in the protection of Claudius and Gertrude, making them responsible for Hamlet's actions.

2. Rosencrantz and Guildenstern come to find out what Hamlet has done with the body of Polonius. He talks in riddles, letting them know that he's buried the body. They come away from the encounter even more convinced that Hamlet is mad.

3. In his letter, Claudius has indicated that the English should kill Hamlet or suffer the consequences for disobeying Claudius' wishes.

4. Hamlet's killing of Polonius pushes Ophelia over the edge to madness. In her mad state, she drowns herself.

5. Claudius draws upon Laertes' desire for revenge of Polonius' murder, the suicide of Ophelia, and Laertes' pride as a swordsman.

Act V

1. The gravedigger and the sexton point out that although Ophelia committed suicide, a mortal sin, as an aristocrat she will receive a Christian burial in the consecrated ground of the cemetery.

2. For Hamlet, the gravedigger has no respect for the dead and makes jokes about them. The gravedigger's humor helps him get through an undesirable task.

3. Hamlet jumps into Ophelia's open grave to show that he loved her as much as Laertes.

4. Hamlet intercepted Claudius' letter while at sea. He now knows that Claudius cannot be trusted and he feels he is justified in killing him.

5. Ironically, Laertes is wounded with his own poisoned weapons after he and Hamlet exchange them in the scuffle. Laertes, realizing that he's wounded mortally, confesses his treachery before dying, so that his soul is not damned eternally.

SUGGESTED ANSWERS FOR
LANGUAGE EXPLORATION ACTIVITIES

Act I: Simile and Metaphor

1. The simile compares the ghost to some guilty being that has been called and is afraid of going, like a puppy called to be punished.

2. The metaphor compares the rooster to a trumpet.

3. The metaphor compares the death of King Hamlet to new plant life or unripened fruit.

4. The metaphor compares Hamlet's disposition to cloudy weather.

5. The metaphor compares Hamlet's mortal body to ice that can melt.

6. For Hamlet, the world is an untended garden, overgrown with weeds.

7. Here, Gertrude's grief over the death of King Hamlet is compared to Niobe's, daughter of Tantalus, who watched Apollo and Artemis slay her seven sons and seven daughters. Watching the horrible sight, she began to cry and, unable to stop, turned to a stone that was always wet with tears.

8. Horatio's simile compares how the ghost looks to how Horatio remembers King Hamlet to look. The appearances of both are as much alike as Horatio's two hands are alike.

9. For Ophelia, the simile compares her brother's advice to a gatekeeper or watchman of her emotions.

10. Ophelia urges her brother to heed his own advice and not be a hypocrite, like some clergy are when they preach austere salvation but engage in excesses themselves.

Act II: Personification and Apostrophe

1. The morning is personified as dressed in a reddish cloak, walking over the hill in the east.

2. Hamlet's agreement to stay is personified as sitting and smiling.

3. Hamlet's apostrophe addresses his heart, the seat of emotions.

4. Polonius personifies wind, allowing it to sit upon the personified shoulder of the sails of the boat.

5. Thoughts are personified as having tongues, and as able to speak themselves.

6. Polonius warns Ophelia not to believe Hamlet's vows of love which he personifies as brokers who encourage unchaste behavior. Polonius suggests that Hamlet may be trying to seduce Ophelia.

7. Hamlet's apostrophe is to all the lost souls who must wander as ghosts.

8. Hamlet's apostrophe is to his uncle Claudius.

9. Fortune is personified, via a reference to the classical goddess Fortune. The First Player also uses an apostrophe to address the gods of Mount Olympus to strike her down, taking her power and destroying her chariot.

10. Hamlet personifies murder as a mute capable of playing a wonderful instrument.

Act III: Symbol

1. Gertrude is a symbol of frailty for Hamlet. The image also echoes the idea of Eve, as woman, being responsible for the downfall of humankind.

2. The baked meats represent the two banquets: served hot at the funeral of King Hamlet, and then served cold at the marriage of Claudius and Gertrude. Hamlet's image suggests that the time between the two ceremonies has been too short.

3. Here the tomb of King Hamlet becomes a symbol for the grave/death as a monster with large, marble jaws that has eaten the body and then spit it out again.

4. The ghost points out that Claudius has, in one act of murder, killed Hamlet's father (life), usurped his position as king (crown), and stolen his wife (queen).

5. Polonius compares the good news that the ambassadors bring to a feast. Polonius' news becomes the fruit that would be served at the end of it.

6. Hamlet uses slings and arrows as symbols for the troubles of life.

7. Death is symbolic sleep.

8. Death is an undiscovered country; no one returns from a journey to it.

9. The candied tongue here represents the sweet words of false flattery.

10. For Claudius, knees represent his willful body and the strings of steel his unrepentant heart.

Act IV: Imagery

1. Appeals to sight; Polonius doesn't want Ophelia to look pale with loneliness.

2. Claudius refers to the pain that comes from being whipped (touch).

3. Ophelia uses an appeal to smell (perfume).

4. Hamlet's curse refers to touch, the coldness of ice and snow, suggesting frigidity.

5. Hamlet's reference is to hearing.

6. Claudius needs to know what he's hearing.

7. The visual simile compares Hamlet's guilt to the pure metal shining within mineral ore.

8. Hamlet's image refers to sight and suggests smell.

9. Claudius uses references to eating (feeds), sight (clouds), and sound (buzzers) to suggest Laertes' desire for revenge.

10. Ophelia's images refer to touch (heat, and the burning of strong salt).

Act V: Irony

1. The verbal irony here revolves around the various meanings of tender: "sincere" as Ophelia uses it; and "as money," attending, and "delivery of self." The last line, "you'll tender me a fool," suggests that the consequence of Ophelia's love for Hamlet will both embarrass Polonius and possibly bring him an illegitimate grandchild.

2. Although Hamlet refers to the revelry of Claudius, the present king, it also refers to the awakening of the dead king, Hamlet's father.

3. Using verbal irony, King Hamlet compares his brother Claudius to a poisonous snake, echoing the image of Satan as the serpent in the Garden of Eden.

4. We don't think of a father wanting anyone to brag about his son's faults.

5. The irony is Hamlet's actions seem to be the prelude to his speaking to her. He doesn't.

6. Claudius asks Rosencrantz and Guildenstern to find out what's bothering Hamlet. Ironically, Hamlet sees through the plan, so they learn nothing but are more convinced of Hamlet's madness.

7. Although Claudius seemed to be praying, he wasn't. Ironically, Hamlet missed his chance to kill him.

8. The verbal irony of the initial exchange between Gertrude and Hamlet turns on *father*. For Gertrude, as Hamlet's mother, Claudius is his father. For Hamlet, King Hamlet is.

9. The verbal irony here turns on Hamlet's use of *king*. The first use is to King Hamlet, who is dead, as is Polonius. The second use is to King Claudius, who doesn't know where Hamlet has buried Polonius' body.

10. The situational irony is that Gertrude drinks poison while celebrating Hamlet's skill as a swordsman.

LANGUAGE EXPLORATION REVIEW

1. B
2. C
3. D
4. D
5. E
6. A
7. D
8. B
9. A
10. E

SUGGESTED ANSWERS FOR VOCABULARY IN CONTEXT

With all these exercises, encourage students to discuss their ideas and interpretations, as their answers will vary. These are suggestions and shouldn't be interpreted as the only valid responses.

Act I

1. Horatio is frightened and in awe of the ghost.

2. King Fortinbras of Norway, father of the character in the play, began a war against Denmark ambitiously and lost.

3. Young Prince Fortinbras has gathered an army together to raid neighboring territories.

4. Hamlet asks Horatio and the others to continue to keep the sighting of the ghost a secret.

5. Laertes announces that all his necessary items have been packed; he's ready to leave for Paris.

6. Laertes warns his sister not to be too willing to believe Hamlet's statements of love.

7. Polonius advises his son that borrowing money is not thrifty.

8. The air on the battlements of the castle is intensely, and perhaps unnaturally, cold.

9. Horatio's response suggests a bitter cold.

10. Hamlet asks the ghost about why it has left its tomb.

Act II

1. Polonius tells Reynaldo to move and listen closer than he would normally to what Laertes' friends say about him.

2. As Polonius continues to instruct Reynaldo, he encourages Reynaldo to tell whatever tales he likes, as long as they don't damage Laertes' reputation in order to gain the confidence of, or find out about Laertes' friends.

3. Coming at the end of Polonius' instructions, Polonius wishes Reynaldo to sound out Laertes' friends to determine whether they're gentlemen or not.

4. Ophelia tells her father that Hamlet came to her with his doublet unfastened, his clothes and appearance in disarray.

5. Ophelia tells her father that Hamlet stared at her, studying her face as though he were going to draw a portrait of her.

6. Claudius encourages Hamlet's school friends to learn what's bothering Hamlet so that he can cure it.

7. Claudius tells Gertrude that Polonius has discovered the source of Hamlet's apparent madness.

8. Polonius confides in the king and queen that he'll send Ophelia to see Hamlet while he eavesdrops behind the tapestry.

9. Hamlet contradicts himself, for he says that he recognizes Polonius and then calls him a fishmonger.

10. Polonius suggests that Hamlet seems obsessed with Ophelia.

Act III

1. Claudius plans to eavesdrop while Ophelia and Hamlet seem to meet by accident.

2. Polonius warns his daughter that evil is often disguised by piety and devotion.

3. Hamlet here sees death as the logical completion and end to the troubles of life.

4. Here, Hamlet uses *mortal coil* to represent the bustle of day-to-day living on earth.

5. Hamlet addresses Ophelia in courtly fashion as though she were some nymph or saint and asks her to remember him in her daily prayers.

6. Hamlet puts a curse on Ophelia if she marries; even if you're as virtuous as ice, as pure as snow, you'll still suffer from a damaged reputation.

7. Hamlet instructs Horatio to watch Claudius during the play and determine if the king reveals his concealed guilt during one speech.

8. The Player Queen states her undying faithfulness to her husband; even if he should die, she will turn aside the advances of suitors.

9. Hamlet tells his mother that Rosencrantz and Guildenstern carry the king's official orders to England.

10. Hamlet knows that Rosencrantz and Guildenstern are ushering him towards trouble.

Act IV

1. Gertrude suggests that Hamlet is as insane as the wind and sea appear to be when they battle each other during a storm.

2. Claudius points out that he and Gertrude will receive blame for Hamlet's murdering Polonius because Hamlet was in their care.

3. Hamlet suggests that dishonest speech goes unquestioned when fools hear it.

4. Claudius points out that the people love Hamlet, so no harm should come to him at present.

5. Claudius suggests that extreme problems need extreme solutions.

6. Fortinbras requests official permission to march his army through Denmark to attack Poland.

7. Claudius suggests that Laertes is not willing to listen to reason regarding his father's death.

8. The gentleman informs the king that the mob calls for Laertes to become king.

9. Claudius wishes to share Laertes' grief.

10. Laertes feels his father was buried without appropriate ceremony, suggesting some dishonor upon Polonius' character.

Act V

1. Hamlet comments upon how entirely disrespectful the gravedigger is of the dead.

2. Hamlet recalls that Yorick, his father's jester, had a lively imagination.

3. Hamlet notices that the order of the funeral procession suggests the person committed suicide and is, therefore, not entitled to all the normal burial rites of the church.

4. Laertes tells the crowd to bury him, the one who's alive, with Ophelia, who's dead.

5. Hamlet challenges Laertes that he is shaming him into also jumping into her open grave.

6. Hamlet points out that people often accidentally learn things that benefit them; events like these suggest that there is divine providence guiding his life.

7. Hamlet emerged from his cabin with his clothes wrapped tightly around him.

8. The image here works on two levels. Using a diminutive of *pack,* Hamlet ironically makes light of a plot to kill him. It also suggests the image of a thief or pickpocket determining the contents of a package by feel or fingering.

9. Hamlet points out that Claudius, like a skilled fisherman, has baited a hook for Hamlet as part of Claudius' usurpation of the throne.

10. As Osric uses *carriages,* he means the carriers that hold the scabbards to belts.

ANSWER KEYS FOR VOCABULARY REVIEW QUIZZES

Act I		Act II		Act III	
1.	D	1.	D	1.	C
2.	B	2.	B	2.	D
3.	A	3.	A	3.	E
4.	C	4.	C	4.	A
5.	A	5.	E	5.	B
6.	E	6.	B	6.	C
7.	B	7.	D	7.	E
8.	B	8.	E	8.	A
9.	A	9.	C	9.	C
10.	E	10.	C	10.	B

Act IV		Act V	
1.	D	1.	A
2.	B	2.	D
3.	B	3.	B
4.	C	4.	C
5.	B	5.	B
6.	E	6.	B
7.	D	7.	C
8.	C	8.	B
9.	A	9.	C
10.	B	10.	B

Appendix D

BIBLIOGRAPHY

Abcarian, Richard and Marvin Klotz, eds. *Literature: The Human Experience.* rev., shorter ed. New York: St. Martin's, 1984.

Allen, Grant and George C. Williamson. *Cities of Northern Italy: Verona, Padua, Bologna, and Ravenna.* Vol. 2. Boston: L. C. Page, 1906.

Barnet, Sylvan, Morton Berman, and William Burto, eds. *An Introduction to Literature: Fiction, Poetry, Drama.* Glenview: Scott, Foresman, 1989.

Bleich, David. *Readings and Feelings: A Guide to Subjective Criticism.* Urbana: National Council of Teachers of English, 1975.

Brockett, Oscar G. *History of the Theatre.* Boston: Allyn and Bacon, 1968.

Brown, Hazel and Brian Cambourne. *Read and Retell: A Strategy for the Whole-Language / Natural Learning Classroom.* Portsmouth: Heinemann, 1987.

Cambourne, Brian. *The Whole Story: Natural Learning and the Acquisition of Literacy in the Classroom.* New York: Ashton-Scholastic, 1989.

Christenbury, Leila and Patricia P. Kelly. *Questioning: A Path to Critical Thinking.* ERIC/RCS Theory and Research into Practice (TRIP) Monograph Series. Urbana: NCTE, 1983.

Davis, James E. and Ronald E. Salomone, eds. *Teaching Shakespeare Today.* Urbana: NCTE, 1993.

Fox, Levi. *William Shakespeare: A Concise Life.* Norwich, England: Jerrold Printing, 1991.

Hamilton, Edith. *Mythology: Timeless Tales of Gods and Heroes.* New York: Mentor Books, 1942.

Lee, Charlotte and David Grote. *Theater: Preparation and Performance.* Glenview: Scott, Foresman, 1982.

Miller, Bruce E. *Teaching the Art of Literature.* Urbana: National Council of Teachers of English, 1980.

Mizner, Arthur, ed. *Teaching Shakespeare: A Guide to the Teaching of Macbeth, Julius Caesar, The Merchant of Venice, Hamlet, Romeo and Juliet, A Midsummer Night's Dream, Othello, As You Like It, Twelfth Night, Richard II, Henry IV, Part One, The Tempest.* New York: The New American Library, Inc., 1969.

Muir, Ramsey. *Muir's Atlas of Ancient & Classical History.* 2nd. ed. New York: Barnes and Noble Inc., 1956.

Robinson, Randal. *Unlocking Shakespeare's Language.* ERIC/RCS Theory and Research into Practice (TRIP) Monograph Series. Urbana: NCTE, 1989.

Rygiel, Mary Ann. Shakespeare Among Schoolchildren: Approaches for the Secondary Classroom. Urbana: NCTE, 1992.

Sisson, Charles Jasper, ed. *Hamlet* in *William Shakespeare: The Complete Works.* New York: Harper & Row, 1953: 999–1042.

Stanford, Judith A. *Responding to Literature.* Mountain View: Mayfield Publishing, 1992.

Vaughn, Joseph L. and Thomas H. Estes. *Reading and Reasoning Beyond the Primary Grades.* Boston: Allyn and Bacon, 1986.

Willek, Rene and Austin Warren. *Theory of Literature.* 3rd ed. New York: Harcourt, Brace & World, Inc., 1970.

Appendix E

VERSIONS OF *HAMLET* AVAILABLE ON VIDEOTAPE

Hamlet. (1948). Laurence Olivier and Jean Simmons. Black and white. 155 minutes.

Hamlet. (1969). Nicol Williamson and Anthony Hopkins. Color. 113 minutes.

Hamlet. (1979). BBC/PBS production for "Shakespeare's Plays" series. Derek Jacobi. Color. 222 minutes.

Rosencrantz and Guildenstern (1990). Richard Dreyfus. Adaptation of Tom Stoppard's stage play that retells the events of *Hamlet* through the eyes of these two characters. Color. 119 minutes.

Availability and Cost:

BBC/PBS versions are available generally through larger video rental chains, state or regional public libraries, or state or regional educational film/media service libraries. Check with your school's librarian or media specialist.

Cost to purchase these video versions range from $25-$100.

The Writing Company issues a special Shakespeare Catalog. Address: 10200 Jefferson Boulevard, Culver City, CA 90232.

All versions listed above are available at present from Filmic Archives, The Cinema Center, Botsford, CT 06404. 1–800–366–1920.